Also Edited by Sondra Kathryn Wilson

*The* Crisis *Reader*

*The* Opportunity *Reader*

*The* Messenger *Reader*

# Lift Every Voice and Sing

# LIFT EVERY VOICE AND SING

*A Celebration of the*
*Negro National Anthem*
*· 100 Years, 100 Voices ·*

Julian Bond and
Sondra Kathryn Wilson,

editors

RANDOM HOUSE
NEW YORK

Library of Congress Cataloging-in-Publication Data is available.
ISBN 0-679-46315-1

Printed in the United States of America on acid-free paper
Random House website address: www.atrandom.com
9 8 7 6 5 4 3 2
First Edition
Book design by Caroline Cunningham

*To the five hundred colored schoolchildren*

*of Jacksonville, Florida, who kept singing*

# ACKNOWLEDGMENTS

Producing *Lift Every Voice and Sing: A Celebration of the Negro National Anthem* has been an inspiring and highly rewarding undertaking.

This book represents the efficacy of consummate publishing professionals: Manie Barron, Melody Guy, and Benjamin Dreyer of Random House. We are exceptionally grateful to them for their spirited efforts, particularly when time was such a critically vital factor; it was imperative that the book's release correspond with the centennial anniversary of "Lift Every Voice and Sing." Manie Barron embraced this project when it was merely an undeveloped proposal. We benefited greatly from his perceptions and sound judgment, which enabled us to truly envision the book. Melody Guy brought a harmonious commitment, accompanied by highly proficient skills, that infused us with the necessary energy to meet the difficult challenges that come with bringing together one hundred voices. Our morale was invariably lifted by her diplomacy and commonsense approach in bringing together individuals who held varying opinions. We were extremely confident in the meticulous editorial skills of Benjamin Dreyer, on whom we relied to produce a work wholly commensurate with our vision down to the last detail.

We were truly blessed to have the wide-ranging assistance of Mildred Bond Roxborough, who became involved in this project in its earliest stages. Her archives proved invaluable as a source for contacting many of the contributors to this book.

Evelyn Parker acted as consulting editor from the beginning of this project. She good-naturedly and with flexibility proffered her time. We will never forget the care and enthusiasm she expressed throughout this endeavor.

We are especially grateful to the mother-and-daughter team of Julie Baker and Angela Baker, of the National Association for the Advancement of Colored People. Serving as liaisons between the editors and the contributors, they never doubted that this objective would be achieved. "It's going to be a great book!" they told us in almost every conversation. We were comforted by their unwavering devotion and ardor.

Our frequent exchanges with Armstrong Williams, from whom we sought advice, were helpful in providing contact information for certain potential contributors; he became one of the project's chief advocates. We came to rely on his insights and his marvelous sense of humor to help the process along in a smooth and timely manner.

Gamilah-L. Shabazz and Nancie Teeter McPhail were helpful in processing information. We will be forever grateful for the sensitivity and compassion they displayed throughout.

We are profoundly indebted to the contributors presented here, who have lifted their voices to celebrate the centennial of "Lift Every Voice and Sing." It is their essays that help relate the profound story of a revered song that has been deeply ingrained in the black experience for generations. It is impossible to find adequate words to convey the significance that each of these individuals has had upon the completion of this book.

We are especially grateful to Ollie Jewel Sims Okala for sharing James Weldon Johnson's correspondence regarding "Lift Every Voice and Sing." We also appreciate the memories she shared of her conversations with James Weldon Johnson about the song. Her help and support have been invaluable to this book.

The pictorial story of African Americans presented here was accomplished with the enthusiastic suggestions and abiding support of Charles L. Blockson, Chris Griffith, Howard Dodson and his staff at Schomburg Center, and Ernie Paniccioli.

We deeply appreciate the generosity of the late Jacob Lawrence, who produced his vision of "Lift Every Voice and Sing" in art form for this book.

This book also represents the assistance of numerous other persons: Yvonne Benjamin, Herb Boyd, A'Lelia Bundles, Lee Daniels, Walter O. Evans, Victoria Horsford, Jennifer Spingarn Huggins, Martin L. Kilson, Honor Spingarn Tranum, Jane White Viazzi, and Craig Stevens Wilson. We benefited from the assistance of countless others; their efforts will not be forgotten.

Finally, we thank our families, who circled us with their love and enthusiasm throughout this process.

# CONTENTS

# INTRODUCTION

I got my first line—*Lift every voice and sing.* Not a startling line, but I worked along grinding out the next five. When, near the end of the first stanza, there came to me the lines

> *Sing a song full of the faith that the dark past has taught us*
> *Sing a song full of the hope that the present has brought us*

the spirit of the poem had taken hold of me. I finished the stanza and turned it over to Rosamond. In composing the two other stanzas I did not use pen and paper. While my brother worked at his musical setting I paced back and forth on the front porch, repeating the lines over and over to myself, going through all of the agony and ecstasy of creating. As I worked through the opening and middle lines of the last stanza:

> *God of our weary years,*
> *God of our silent tears,*
> *Thou who hast brought us thus far on our way;*
> *Thou who hast by Thy might*
> *Led us into the light.*
> *Keep us forever in the path, we pray.*
> *Lest our feet stray from the places, our God, where we met Thee,*
> *Lest, our hearts, drunk with the wine of the world, we forget*
> > *Thee . . .*

I could not keep back the tears, and made no effort to do so. I was experiencing the transports of the poet's ecstasy. Feverish ecstasy was followed by that contentment—that sense of serene joy—which makes artistic creation the most complete of all human experiences. When I had put the last stanza down on paper I at once recognized the Kiplingesque touch in the two longer lines quoted above; but I knew that in the stanza the American Negro was, historically and spiritually, immanent; and I decided to let it stand as it was written.*

—JAMES WELDON JOHNSON

It is wondrous and hardly explicable to many how James Weldon Johnson could have written such spiritually enriching lyrics in 1900 despite the restraints ordained by Jim Crow laws, despite frenzied lynchings and mob violence, despite the fact that white America had established an educational system teeming with stereotypes that had misrepresented and malformed virtually every external view of African American life. Underpinning these sweeping injustices was the Supreme Court's ruling in the infamous *Plessy v. Ferguson* case four years before "Lift Every Voice and Sing" was written in 1900. This decision meant that state laws requiring "separate but equal" facilities for African Americans were a "reasonable" use of state powers. Further, "The object of the [Fourteenth] Amendment was undoubtedly to enforce the absolute equality of the two races before the laws, but in the nature of things it could not have been intended to abolish distinctions based on color, or to enforce social, as distinguished from political, equality, or a commingling of the two races upon terms unsatisfactory to either."†

"Lift Every Voice and Sing" is fittingly provocative. Yet its message, ingeniously crafted, does not fuel the fires of racial hatred.

*James Weldon Johnson, *Along This Way: The Autobiography of James Weldon Johnson.* New York: Viking Press, 1933, pp. 154–155.
†Lerone Bennett, Jr., *Before the Mayflower: A History of Black America.* New York: Penguin Books, 1988, p. 267.

Sociologist E. Franklin Frazier pointed out that in "Lift Every Voice and Sing," James Weldon Johnson endowed the African American enslavement and struggle for freedom with a certain nobility. Frazier further noted that Johnson expressed an acceptance of the past and confidence in the future. It is likely that Johnson was attempting to cultivate a sense of history among his race. On the one hand, the lyrics reveal how African Americans were estranged from their cultural past by the impact of racial oppression and that they manifested the psychological and physical scars inflicted by that injustice. On the other hand, the song is irrefutably one of the most stalwart and inspiring symbols in American civil rights history. Not wanting African Americans to lose hope, James Weldon Johnson included in the lyrics none of his pragmatic reservations regarding justice for his race. His enriching directive is assuredly one of the mainstays of the song's mastery and endurance. Notwithstanding, he tells us in "Lift Every Voice and Sing" that we must persist—we must remain vigilant until victory is won.

To understand how James Weldon Johnson conceived and produced such motivating lyrics when white supremacy served as the backdrop of virtually every phase of black life, one has to comprehend his beliefs and experiences, so clearly evident in the "everlasting" song he called "the Negro National Hymn." In the lyrics we see his unswerving self-confidence and optimism, his faith in African Americans, and his strong belief that the then existing system, a counterfeit representation of the United States Constitution, could not endure.

Johnson's self-confidence and optimism are easily discernible in his early life. As a boy he staunchly proclaimed that he wanted one day to be the governor of his home state of Florida. His parents, James and Helen Dillet Johnson, had instilled in him and in his younger brother, J. Rosamond Johnson, such a sanguine view of America that the boys surely believed that whatever their young minds could conceive, they could achieve. During his early years, James believed himself beneficiary to all the privileges afforded any American who desired to develop his full potential. But while attending Atlanta University, he came to understand that the Jim

Crow system did not allow status or individual liberation for African Americans, no matter what they achieved. This harsh realization enabled him to see through the deception of white supremacy. He was determined to acknowledge the effects of racism, but he was even more resolved not to internalize them. Therefore, his innate optimism remained firmly intact. "Lift Every Voice and Sing" illustrates James Weldon Johnson's understanding of the existing system as well as his confidence in the future. His determination to remain spiritually unfettered by the effects of racism is evident in the following pledge he wrote.

> *I will not allow one prejudiced person or one million or one hundred million to blight my life. I will not let prejudice or any of its attendant humiliations and injustices bear me down to spiritual defeat. My inner life is mine, and I shall defend and maintain its integrity against all the powers of hell.* *

His confidence in his race is unmistakably personified in "Lift Every Voice and Sing." This faith in the family of race was reinforced during his college years and while teaching in the backwoods of Georgia. As a student at Atlanta University during the late nineteenth century, James Weldon Johnson recognized that the subject of race was almost invariably the topic of debates, speeches, and essays. He acknowledged, "The atmosphere was charged with it. Nearly all that was acquired, mental and moral, was destined to be fitted into a particular system, of which race was the center."

His teaching experience in rural Henry County, Georgia, the summer following his freshman year of college, proved to be a momentous spiritual and educational manifestation. It was here, where the adversarial relations between black and white were flagrant and inescapable, that he was introduced to the crude dimensions of racism. Through this experience, he accepted that his people had been obstructed for centuries by prejudice, intolerance, and brutality, and hobbled by their own ignorance, poverty, and

---

*James Weldon Johnson, *Negro Americans, What Now?* New York: Viking Press, 1934, p. 102.

helplessness. Nonetheless, he believed, in the face of this weighty burden they remained courageous and unvanquished. This hopefulness, he wrote, was evidenced in their capacity to fervently *sing* of a better day. Writing about his newfound faith and pride in his people, he contended, "I laid the first stones in the foundation of faith in them on which I have stood ever since."[*]

Resolving that the race problem was paradoxical, he wrote that white America's superior status was not always real, but often imaginary and artificially bolstered by bigotry and buttressed by the forces of injustice.[†] Asserting that this false position could not infinitely defy the truth, he reasoned that white America's belief in its mental, moral, and physical superiority was specious. Knowing that the American system of democracy was deceptive, and believing that many white Americans realized this fact also, he was moved to proclaim, "Undoubtedly, some people will find it difficult to understand why a supremacy of which we have heard so much, a supremacy which claims to be based upon congenital superiority, should require such drastic methods of protection."[‡]

As a college student, Johnson had realized the glaring contradictions between white America's actions and the true aims of the United States Constitution. He believed that the Constitution meant exactly what it said, and it was his inexorable faith in the founding principles of America that inspired him to write "Lift Every Voice and Sing" not as an anthem but as a hymn. He did not conceive the song as an anthem, and at no time did he refer to it in that manner. By the 1920s the song was being pasted inside the back covers of hymnal books across the South and in many parts of the North. It is likely that around this time the "anthem" label evolved through folklore, thus sealing the song's permanent status among African Americans as their "Negro National Anthem."

James Weldon Johnson was the chief executive officer of the NAACP during the 1920s, when the organization made "Lift Every

[*]James Weldon Johnson, *Along This Way*, pp. 119–120.
[†]Ibid.
[‡]See James Weldon Johnson's *New York Age* editorial, "Anglo-Saxon in Mississippi" (December 3, 1914).

Voice and Sing" its "official song." Because of his strong belief that "a nation can have but one anthem" and the NAACP's fundamental ideology of integration, labeling the song an "anthem" would have been antithetical to the organization's central objective. Johnson's main task as NAACP leader was to legally abolish the fiendish acts of lynchings that were increasingly occurring; he called for the saving of black America's bodies and white America's souls. He certainly understood that when the wide-ranging forces of racism struck, his people needed something to fall back on. And it was clear to him that African Americans made the song what they needed it to be—their anthem of hope and prayer.

. . .

We present in this volume essays by one hundred Americans who discuss the importance of "Lift Every Voice and Sing" in their lives; many have included statements on the subject of race in America. These one hundred contributors include legislators, politicians, educators, writers, and performers. Their essays build a multifaceted narrative that elucidates the value and profundity of a song that has vibrantly endured for one hundred years.

We have also included a panoply of one hundred photographs that span the twentieth century and offer a view of the rich and diverse experiences of a people as they pursue justice in our nation.

# LIFT EVERY VOICE AND SING

*James Weldon Johnson (standing) and J. Rosamond Johnson, c. 1920s.* Courtesy of ASCAP

A group of young men in Jacksonville, Florida, arranged to celebrate Lincoln's birthday in 1900. My brother, J. Rosamond Johnson, and I decided to write a song to be sung at the exercise. I wrote the words and he wrote the music. Our New York publisher, Edward B. Marks, made mimeographed copies for us and the song was taught to and sung by a chorus of five hundred colored school children.

Shortly afterwards my brother and I moved from Jacksonville to New York, and the song passed out of our minds. But the school children of Jacksonville kept singing it, they went off to other schools and sang it, they became teachers and taught it to other children. Within twenty years it was being sung over the South and in some other parts of the country. Today, the song, popularly known as the Negro National Hymn, is quite generally used.

The lines of this song repay me in elation, almost of exquisite anguish, whenever I hear them sung by Negro children.

—JAMES WELDON JOHNSON, 1935

## Lift Every Voice and Sing

*Lift every voice and sing*
*Till earth and heaven ring,*
*Ring with the harmonies of Liberty;*
*Let our rejoicing rise*
*High as the listening skies,*

*Let it resound loud as the rolling seas.*
*Sing a song full of the faith that the dark past has taught us,*
*Sing a song full of the hope that the present has brought us,*
*Facing the rising sun of our new day begun,*
*Let us march on till victory is won.*

*Stony the road we trod,*
*Bitter the chastening rod,*
*Felt in the days when hope unborn had died;*
*Yet with a steady beat,*
*Have not our weary feet*
*Come to the place for which our fathers sighed?*
*We have come over a way that with tears has been watered,*
*We have come treading our path through the blood of the*
    *slaughtered,*
*Out from the gloomy past,*
*Till now we stand at last*
*Where the white gleam of our bright star is cast.*

*God of our weary years,*
*God of our silent tears,*
*Thou who hast brought us thus far on the way;*
*Thou who has by Thy might*
*Led us into the light.*
*Keep us forever in the path, we pray.*
*Lest our feet stray from the places, our God, where we met*
    *Thee,*
*Lest our hearts, drunk with the wine of the world, we forget*
    *Thee,*
*Shadowed beneath Thy hand,*
*May we forever stand,*
*True to our God*
*True to our native land.*

WORDS BY JAMES WELDON JOHNSON

MUSIC BY J. ROSAMOND JOHNSON

# 100 Years, 100 Voices

# BILLYE AARON

retired executive, United Negro College Fund

# HANK AARON

retired professional baseball player

When President Abraham Lincoln issued his Emancipation Proclamation some 138 years ago, it set in motion an ongoing struggle for
African Americans to make real the promise of America.

The road to freedom, justice, and equality has been for us a
long and treacherous one, replete with detours and dead ends, but
with no rest stops and no discernible signboards.

Yet, in spite of all the roadblocks, as a people we have been able
to rise above the inhumanity of slavery and the deprivation and humiliation of segregation and discrimination and embrace the dignity and destiny of democracy. So that today, one hundred years
after James Weldon Johnson and J. Rosamond Johnson's "Lift
Every Voice and Sing," our people have remained "true to our native land."

Feeling passionately as we do about this song, we salute and pay
homage to the memory and contributions of the Johnsons. Their
collaboration gave us a song that no doubt will be sung through the
ages by generations to come, with the same dignity and pride that
we feel when we sing it today. We hope that it will inspire them as
it has inspired us to give back to our communities and support
those causes that enhance opportunities for our children.

"Lift Every Voice and Sing" also touches our hearts because it
speaks directly to us and to our people. It belongs to us—was written for us—is sung by us.

We celebrate and commemorate the creative genius of the
Johnsons and thank God for the gift of their powerful lyrics and
reverent melody. We see in their song a tie that binds all of us as
African Americans together. Our history and our heritage enable

*Mr. and Mrs. Edward Sims of North Little Rock, Arkansas, 1900.* Courtesy of The James Weldon Johnson Collection, Ollie Jewel Sims Okala, and Sondra Kathryn Wilson

us—empower us—to be strong and always, always, to continue the struggle for justice and equality for our people.

We carry this commitment into the new millennium knowing that the gains made in the courts and by presidential mandates are eroding. Even now, after 243 years of the "worst form of slavery the world has ever known" and 138 years of segregation and racial discrimination, thirty-five-year-old affirmative action is being dismantled and abandoned.

And so we recommend "Lift Every Voice and Sing" to every black American. Learn the words! Sing the song! Be inspired! Support worthy organizations such as the NAACP, the NAACP Legal Defense and Education Fund, the Urban League, the Southern Christian Leadership Conference, and the United Negro College Fund—all venerable organizations that have kept the faith and kept their hands on the plow. We should rally around them and all worthy black causes that lift up our people—at the ballot box, in the boardroom, and wherever the spirit of racism resides. For indeed, we must "march on till victory is won."

"Lift Every Voice and Sing" has kept us grounded—connected to our yesterday, mindful of our today, and hopeful for our tomorrow.

## Maya Angelou

poet, scholar, and producer

Stamps is a dusty little hamlet in southwest Arkansas, twenty-five miles from Texas and thirty miles from Hope, the birthplace of the forty-second president of the United States. I was three years old in 1931, when I was sent from Los Angeles, California, to Stamps.

My brother Bailey and I were students at Lafayette County Training School, the first- through tenth-grade academic institution for black students. Every day the routine was the same: all classes gathered in the auditorium at eight A.M. There, a chosen student would unfurl the flag and standing, each person with right hand on left breast would recite the preamble to the U.S. Constitution in one voice with three breaths; then we would sing the National Anthem (when no adults were looking, we would continue the line "O, say, can you see" by singing "any bedbugs on me?"). Then finishing that song and in the same key, standing on the same leg, we sang "Lift Every Voice and Sing." Everybody I knew, or met, knew "Lift Every Voice and Sing." I don't think anyone thought about the lyrics, certainly not my brother, or I, or any kids we knew.

Then the black community arranged itself excitedly to celebrate. Children trembled visibly with anticipation. I was the person of the moment because I was graduating from grammar school. It was very important. Even white folks would attend the ceremony, and one would speak of God and the Southern way of life. We started the program as usual with the National Anthem and went straight into "Lift Every Voice and Sing." Then our principal introduced Mr. Edward Don Leavy, who arrived at the podium, looked at the audience once, and stepped into his speech. He told us of the wonderful changes in store for the children in Stamps. The Central School (where white children were enrolled) would have a well-known artist from Little Rock to teach them and the newest microscopes and chemistry equipment to teach them. He said Lafayette County Training School (the black school) would have the only colored paved playing field in that part of Arkansas and our home economics building would be upgraded. A number of heads were bowed down and our parents and grandparents refused to look at us. We would study home economics so that we could become better maids; we would play ball so that we could become better handymen.

Don Leavy left the stage with a cursory good-bye and all of a sudden I looked up and saw Henry Reed, the conservative, the proper, the A student, turn his back to the audience and turn to us (the proud graduating class of 1940) and sing, nearly speaking.

> *Lift every voice and sing*
> *Till earth and heaven ring*
> *Ring with the harmonies of Liberty . . .*

It was the poem written by James Weldon Johnson. It was the music composed by J. Rosamond Johnson. It was the Negro National Anthem. Out of habit, we were singing it.

Our mothers and fathers stood in the dark hall and joined the hymn of encouragement.

> *Stony the road we trod,*
> *Bitter the chastening rod,*
> *Felt in the days when hope unborn had died;*
> *Yet with a steady beat,*
> *Have not our weary feet*
> *Come to the place for which our fathers sighed?*

I personally had never heard them before. Never heard the words, despite the thousands of times I had sung them. Never thought they had anything to do with me.

And now I heard, really for the first time:

> *We have come over a way that with tears has been watered,*
> *We have come treading our path through the blood of the*
> *     slaughtered.*

While echoes of the song shivered in the air, Henry Reed bowed his head, said thank you, and returned to his place in the line. The tears that slipped down many faces were not wiped away in shame.

We were on top again. As always, again. We survived. The depths had been icy and dark, but now a bright sun spoke to our souls. I was no longer simply a member of the proud graduating class, I was a proud member of the wonderful, beautiful Negro race.

Oh, black known and unknown poets, how often have your auctioned pains sustained us? Who will compute the lonely nights made less lonely by your songs, or the empty pots made less tragic by your poems?

*Jack Johnson (left), the first black heavyweight champion, in a match against Sam McVey, 1903.* Courtesy of Schomburg Center for Research in Black Culture, The New York Public Library

# AMIRI BARAKA

poet, scholar, and playwright

"Lift Every Voice and Sing" was part of my growing up. Very early in my expanding perception I understood that at certain programs my parents took me to, the Negro National Anthem would be sung. The National Association of Postal Employees gatherings; dances, conventions, meetings, &c. When we went down to Tuskegee, where my mother had attended normal school, and I saw a statue of Booker T. Washington pulling the cover of ignorance off the prototype slave, there was the anthem loud and heartfelt.

At a few gatherings in Newark, at Bethany Baptist and some other churches (for special programs, e.g. Roland Hayes, Philippa Schuyler), the (Howard University) Alumni House, the Colored YMCAs, the Terrace Ballroom, programs held by my mother's various clubs (e.g., the Girl Friends), at soirees, it might be a benefit for the NAACP or Urban League, or the black community hospital, or my grandfather's black Republican meetings, my grandmother's American Woodsmen sets (an Afro-American insurance company) and Poro(!) programs of black beauticians, the anthem usually ended the event.

When we went down to Tennessee, to visit Fisk, where she'd gone to college, where there were also those dynamite murals by Aaron Douglass I remembered all my life, "Lift Every Voice" was sung, further animating that gathering with the heap of heavy vibrations from the folks I saw and, I felt, black angels hovering invisibly, rah rah ing the proceedings.

At gatherings like this, I was reached deep down throughout my self. A feeling of some still not completely identified "We-ness" . . . that we black folks were actually real and had desires independent of the lunacy of the vicious racist white folks I was told about every few evenings at the dinner table. Tales, events, ongoing commentary on the bestiality of American apartheid and the struggle and travails, including lynchings present and past, remembered and talked about, of the Afro-American people.

As a child, certainly, I took all this in. And it bottomed in me as a kind of base, a foundation of humanity sought. A map and diagram, a historic journey laid out from which I would draw on always. So I had deepness given to me, throughout my childhood, that we were "colored people," that we were suffering unjust, uncivilized, un-Christian, even maniacal treatment by ignorant, evil "jealous crackers." The last, my grandmother always ended with, in memory of my grandfather's two burned-up grocery stores and threatened funeral parlor in Dothan, Alabama. Where my family finally had to flee, terrorized by Klan-like forces who threatened to kill them all, for the crime of self-determination, an openly strived for socioeconomic advance, and stubbornly husbanded dignity.

When we went back to Dothan, on the Tuskegee trip, I heard about the past from some old, near-dead, red-faced mummies sitting in a grocery store, who opinioned that I "talked too clear" at age seven or eight. I'm sure the older Joneses took my almost falling into a well, after the dead people's "playback," as an omen of the death threat still hanging over the place.

No doubt the bitterness of the small black petty bourgeoisie, driven from the black belt to Beaver Falls (near Pittsburgh) and finally to open a store in Newark, N.J., where shortly after, the depression put my grandfather out of business . . . was also part of my socialization and slowly crystallizing consciousness. Hearing "Lift Every Voice" seemed always to give me a sweeping recall of everything I'd been told and even witnessed (the dirty colored car of the segregated trains to the south; the balcony colored section, reached by rickety side stairs, of the movie; the crazed reaction to my seven-year-old speech; my mother, one day, in Newark, cussing out a white storekeeper for calling the nuts she was buying "nigger toes": "Those are Brazil nuts, lady!" Then stalking off, whipping little me behind her as she exited on fire.

But the song had a blossoming beauty to it. The words began to deepen in me over the years. What my consciousness had grasped as literal meaning was also given a heavier gravity by the emotional opening the words carried with them. A direct access to the "true self-consciousness" Du Bois speaks of. That there was a beauty to

*Ada Overton Walker and George Walker in dance costume, 1905.* Courtesy of Schomburg Center for Research in Black Culture, The New York Public Library

us, a dignity, a strength, untouched by the acknowledged Ugly American national oppression, its robbery, denial of rights, slander, repression, violence, murder. That we existed independent of that, somehow, that our "humanity" was as real as we were, and could not be damaged by the devil himself.

Even today that feeling remains, every time I hear the anthem. It's why I included it in a "Word Music" work my wife, Amina, and our group, Blue Ark, do often called "Funk Lore: Black History Music," where we perform a ninety-minute overview of Afro-American history and the music that is its cultural chronology, from the Middle Passage to Malcolm, ending with my wife's great poem about Malcolm X, backed by the anthem. It provides a stunning denouement, summing up black history as a living being, still struggling for Self-determination, Equal Citizenship Rights, and Democracy!

"Lift Every Voice" must be acknowledged as James Weldon Johnson and Rosamond Johnson's greatest work (pace "Black and Unknown Bards" and "The Creation") because it is not only exquisite poetry but a lyric whose aesthetic dialectic uncovers and releases deep historic and ennobling experience from within itself, swinging joyously into ourselves, triggered by our singing. (In this sense, it is truly the highest form of a People's Poetry!) As if our voices were the only necessary ingredient to be added so that we can actually rise, soar, and become, for that expression's duration, that "band of angels" in the chariot, ourselves, and when returned to earth, more strongly aware that our task is to carry ourselves "home," that is, to continue the historic revolutionary democratic struggle to transform this Heathen Hell into a dwelling fit for evolving Humanity.

*W. W. Booker of Wilmot, Arkansas, with his daughter Ruth, Christmas, 1915.* Courtesy of Evelyn Barnes
Parker

# HARRY BELAFONTE

entertainer

"Lift Every Voice and Sing," one of the most momentous sociological and literary achievements at the onset of the twentieth century, has markedly affected my life and work by virtue of its implication that the role of art isn't just to show life as it is but to show life as it should be. In this sacred song James Weldon Johnson fused the sufferings, pathos, hopes, and dreams of a people to create an enduring and material work of art. In essence, "Lift Every Voice and Sing" symbolizes the power of combining art with the human struggle. It is a glorious song that carries a mighty social message of a race's "gloomy past" and its hope for a promising future. Johnson writes: "*Sing a song full of the faith that the dark past has taught us, / Sing a song full of the hope that the present has brought us, / Facing the rising sun of our new day begun, / Let us march on till victory is won.*" Like Johnson's social and political interests, mine have been and remain central to the development of my art. Accordingly, variable human travails are most likely reflected in my songs and other art forms. This concept of merging human issues with art evolved in my adolescent years during a stay on the island of Jamaica.

I was born in Harlem, in New York City. Since I was impressionable and vulnerable to the wrong influences in Harlem, my mother believed the island of her birth, Jamaica, was a safer place for me to spend my early adolescence. During these years, I worked at various odd jobs. Labor was cheap and life in general was difficult, because of the economic and social inequities that permeated Jamaican life. Many of my songs were anomalous in that they sprang out of the difficult conditions of my environment. Further, this early experience helped to expand my artistic range by enabling me to transmute aspects of the human rights struggle into creations like my song "Day-O."

The dual message of the dark past of slavery and of hope in "Lift Every Voice and Sing" embodies the African American experience in this nation. As we begin this new century, I vow to continue to blend art and human rights to make a better world, with God's grace.

# Derrick Bell

law professor, New York University

Nostalgia has its place. We would be dangerously remiss, however, if we failed in observing the centennial of "Lift Every Voice and Sing" to make a serious comparison between the terrible plight of blacks in 1900, the year that James Weldon Johnson and his brother, J. Rosamond, wrote the song, and the more subtle but strangely similar dangers our people face today.

The historian Rayford W. Logan described the period in which the Johnsons worked as the "nadir" for black people. His depiction was not extravagant. It defined the depths to which blacks were reduced, and the nature of the betrayal and brutality which brought the freedmen low. The by then half-century-old curse of the Dred Scott decision, namely that "blacks had no rights that whites were bound to respect," retained its validity in practice, one that the law ignored.

The racial segregation approved by the Supreme Court four years earlier, in 1896, must have seemed the least of the racist outrages visited arbitrarily on a people excluded from the vote and trapped in menial jobs and a sharecrop system hardly better than slavery. In addition, there was the constant danger. A black man's life could be taken on a white man's whim. Neither industriousness nor deference necessarily protected a black from summary execution by lynching if whites suspected one of us harbored dangerous tendencies or if they felt he or she was acting like a "smart-assed" nigger who needed chastisement.

The immediate popularity of "Lift Every Voice," and its longevity, attest to the encouragement and renewed faith it brought to a people who, as the old hymn puts it, "Been in the Storm So

*Members of the NAACP-sponsored Amenia Conference, held at Troutbeck, the country estate of NAACP board member J. E. Spingarn, in Amenia, New York, August 1916.* Photo by James Weldon Johnson; courtesy of The James Weldon Johnson Collection, Ollie Jewel Sims Okala, and Sondra Kathryn Wilson

Long." There are, then, reasons grounded in respect and recognition to sing "Lift Every Voice and Sing" with gratitude on this its hundredth anniversary. One would have hoped, though, that its spiritual enrichment as well as our status as outsiders suggested by its adoption as the "Negro National Anthem" would by now be a matter for the archives of memory.

True, there is today a black presence in a great many areas of American life, and yet the glitter of those gains is overshadowed by the continued disparity between whites and blacks in virtually every measure of well-being. The pressures of modern life, including, of course, continuing racial bias, are destroying all too many black families, with the fallout of that destruction manifested in the shocking percentages of our young men condemned to long years in prison, and our young women (girls, really) trapped in too-early parenthood. Discrimination is now harder to prove in court, but no less real. It functions as a marker of continued subordination, while it handicaps opportunity and undermines self-confidence.

Progress, to the extent it has occurred, has provided individual opportunity for advancement for a great many of us, but our "moving on up" renders our communities more vulnerable to the hostility that lies just below the surface in much of America. Rather than models for our less well off, we who too quickly have been deemed to have "made it" find ourselves isolated at the workplace and in our communities. All too frequently, we assume—as did the Jews in pre-Nazi Germany—that our success is a guarantee of our security. It is not.

The readiness of all too many whites to sacrifice black people on the altar of their white privilege has not much changed. Americans in name, we remain in jeopardy in fact. If the economy fails, we are in trouble. If those on the far right achieve the majority power they seek, our fortunes will decline precipitously. If there is even one outrageous incident for which one of us is deemed the cause, the retaliation will be swift and indiscriminate.

The threat is real. Just imagine if any one—and Lord help us if more than one—of these mass executions of unarmed children and their teachers had been planned and carried out, not by privileged white students, but by black kids retaliating for the alienation and rejection they experience every day of their lives. There would be no descriptive term too awful to describe the retaliatory violence we would encounter, working, middle, and upper-class alike.

In response, we can sing "Lift Every Voice" with ever more vigor. It must, though, serve as prelude to dedication as individuals and groups, and not an assumption that the music, inspiring though it is, will alone insure that those who succeed us will be able to celebrate the centennial of the Johnson brothers' fine song.

## MARILYN BERGMAN

president, American Society of Composers, Authors, and Publishers (ASCAP)

It's a true privilege to have been asked to contribute my thoughts to this volume celebrating the centennial of the legendary "Lift Every Voice and Sing." First, the song has great meaning for us at ASCAP because it is the best-known work by the incredibly gifted and prolific brothers James Weldon Johnson and J. Rosamond Johnson, both of whom were pioneering members of ASCAP. James was, in fact, one of two African Americans who were charter members of ASCAP, joining in 1914 (the other was composer Harry T. Burleigh). Second, the timeless beauty, inspiring message, and uninterrupted popularity of "Lift Every Voice" make it one of our culture's most treasured works. And, of course, the song's status as the "Negro National Anthem" and its long connection with the NAACP make the centennial of "Lift Every Voice" most worthy of recognition by the association.

I have long been aware of James Weldon Johnson's stature as one of America's leading poets. But in doing further reading, I was interested to learn that he and his brother were active in the early-twentieth-century New York show business world, participating in vaudeville and other theatrical efforts. The versatile Johnsons were leaders of the Harlem Renaissance, the twentieth century's first

*In response to an East St. Louis race riot, the NAACP sponsored a silent protest march on Fifth Avenue, New York City, July 28, 1917.* Courtesy of Schomburg Center for Research in Black Culture, The New York Public Library

flowering of art, music, and dance in New York's African American community. But, like songwriters in every modern era, the Johnsons met with publishers and sought to place their songs before the public in any way they could. Among their "firsts" was being the first black writers (with their friend and collaborator Bob Cole) to score a Broadway musical with a white cast (*Humpty Dumpty,* in 1902). Rosamond Johnson later became the first black composer to score a feature film (*The Emperor Jones,* 1933).

The Johnson brothers composed "Lift Every Voice and Sing" in early 1900 for a Lincoln's Birthday observance in their hometown of Jacksonville, Florida. That was only thirty-five years after the end of the Civil War, in a former slave state, at a time when Jim Crow laws, lynchings, and other racial injustices were a daily fact of life. James Weldon Johnson's lyrics do not prettify past abuses; rather, they speak poetically to the agonies and crimes that were visited upon his people. However, instead of despair, Johnson's words offer spiritual renewal, healing, and bright hope. It is a song of vision, a prelude in many ways to the unforgettable "I have a dream" speech which electrified our nation sixty years later. We at ASCAP salute James Weldon Johnson and J. Rosamond Johnson for their towering achievement and commend our friends at the NAACP for this marvelous tribute to their classic song.

## CHARLES BLOCKSON

curator, The Charles L. Blockson Afro-American Collection, Temple University

Over many years as a collector of books and other artifacts of African American history and culture, I have often been moved to tears, laughter, deep reflection, pride, even anger and rage. Many years ago, I recall the shock and amazement that surged through me as I held a piece of early-twentieth-century sheet music in an antiques shop. The music included a statement that "every race has a song but the negro." Stereotyping of this sort was, of course, not

*Lieutenant Marion R. Perry, Jr., c. 1918.* Courtesy of The Walker Family Collection, A'Lelia
Bundles

uncommon during that period of American history. As a young man coming of age in the 1940s and 1950s, I also knew that cultural fare of this type still accurately reflected some attitudes toward Americans of African descent.

Like most African American bibliophiles, I have made a habit of collecting materials that reflect moments and events evoking both the pride and prejudice of American society with regard to race. Just about a year after adding the aforementioned piece of racist sheet music to my collection, I found myself going through another batch of sheet music at a used-book store I had discovered while in New York City participating in an indoor track meet. My eye was caught by sheet music for a song by two African American composers. It was the music and lyrics to James Weldon Johnson and J. Rosamond Johnson's "Lift Every Voice and Sing."

As I read through the piece, I felt my soul awash with relief and refreshing inspiration. It revived my soul to hold a piece of the evidence that, in spite of all the negatives, this revered rejoinder had been accomplished by these two brothers, who were very young at the time of their lasting creation. Ironically, "Lift Every Voice," also known as the Negro National Anthem, had been written roughly around the same time as the piece I had purchased the year before.

I grew up what might seem at first glance to be a world away from the Deep South: in Norristown, Pennsylvania, the county seat of Montgomery County, eighteen miles from Philadelphia, and, unlike my Southern brothers and sisters, I attended predominantly white schools. Still, the racism of the South was pervasive in the North as well. I had been unaware of the existence of the song "Lift Every Voice and Sing" as a child. It simply wasn't available to us. Like millions of African American schoolchildren nationwide, I had grown accustomed to singing "The Star-Spangled Banner" each morning as the only "National Anthem" I knew. Even at an early age, however, I felt uncomfortable singing "The Star-Spangled Banner," which I later learned had been written by Francis Scott Key, who actually adapted the tune from "To Anacreon in Heaven," a popular drinking song sung in British taverns of the day.

In 1955, during my years as a scholarship athlete at Penn State, singing that anthem really weighed on me as I stood solemnly on the pregame ceremony sidelines with my football teammates Jesse Arnelle, Lenny Moore, and Rosey Grier. That same year, Emmett Till had been brutally lynched in Mississippi. As the university band played "The Star-Spangled Banner" and tens of thousands of voices rose, I soothed my soul and offered balm to my consciousness by humming "Lift Every Voice and Sing." Though we were thousands of miles away, my heart and soul, and those of African American athletes across the country, said many quiet prayers for the brave youth of the South: for the children of Birmingham and Montgomery, Nashville and Greensboro; for the Freedom Riders and the marchers. Though I was unable to be with them, I could give voice to our solidarity in a small way by humming "Lift Every Voice and Sing."

Let us march on into the twenty-first century carrying high the pride and determination that our ancestors, upon whose shoulders we stand, bequeathed to us. My life has been spent in an attempt to preserve the record of the history of that struggle. As long as I have the record of our struggle, the words and images and signs, to comfort me, I will continue, as must we all. It is important that all African Americans preserve a bit of our birthright of pride and struggle by singing this sacred song. As it has from the first time I heard it and countless times since, "Lift Every Voice and Sing" constantly revives my soul.

## JULIA W. BOND

retired educator

My husband, the late Dr. Horace Mann Bond, and I were fortunate to have known James Weldon Johnson. During the early 1930s, James Weldon Johnson and my husband were professors at Fisk University in Nashville, Tennessee. In those days Jim Crow barred African Americans from using local parks or other recreational facilities in Nashville. My grandmother Callie Browne lived at 503

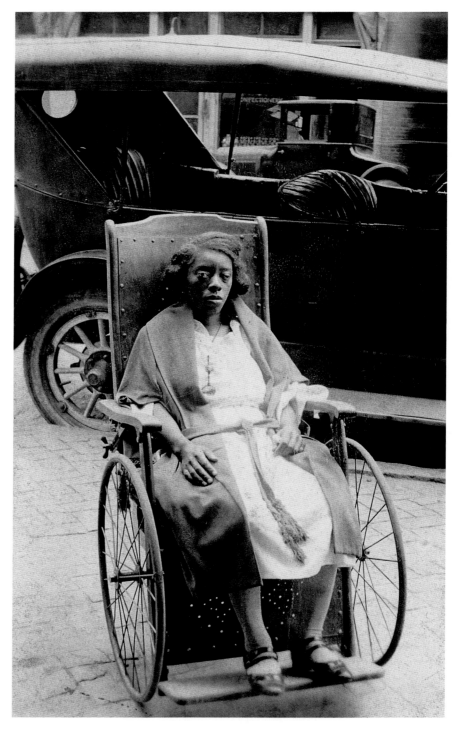

*A wheelchair-bound woman, c. 1919.* Courtesy of The Charles L. Blockson Afro-American
Collection, Temple University

Mile End in Nashville. Her large house, set in the midst of grounds that were covered with blooms, became the place where some of the city's African American residents gathered on Sunday afternoons. Fisk University professors like James Weldon Johnson, E. Franklin Frazier, Alrutheus Taylor, Charles S. Johnson, and their families were among our frequent guests. By this time, "Lift Every Voice and Sing" was widely sung in the African American community, particularly in the South, and it had been adopted by the NAACP as its official song.

When I think of songs of the civil rights movement, it is "Lift Every Voice and Sing" that comes to mind. Moreover, it was beautifully written by the Johnson brothers for almost every occasion.

Early on I instinctively understood that the song's message held great promise and was an important theme in the struggle for freedom. At home, church, and school, we sang the song with a unique enthusiasm that brought each word to life. While singing, we stood tall and held our heads high with pride and dignity.

Writing about "Lift Every Voice and Sing," which chronicles in song the black struggle, I am reminded of something my husband wrote more than fifty years ago: "The estate of the scholar is an ancient and honorable one, known of olden times, and in each generation, even in times of distress and human misery and wretchedness, a refuge and a haven for the souls of men."

## MATTYE TOLLETTE BOND

retired educator

In 1893, the United States Postal Service granted my father permission to establish a post office at a rural Arkansas crossroads. The official name of the designated post office was Tollette—my father's surname. The Tollette post office became the center of the town he then founded. Father served as postmaster, assisted by my mother. Upon his death in 1898, my mother became postmistress.

After my birth in 1895, my mother regularly carried me to the

*Madam C. J. Walker, entrepreneur and philanthropist, meeting with businessmen and (far left) labor activist and civil rights pioneer A. Philip Randolph, c. 1919.* Courtesy of The Walker Family Collection, A'Lelia Bundles

post office, which was a two-room structure built by the crossroads in front of our property. During the day, she would read to me from various publications received in the mail. There she also taught me to read. By 1906, I had become an avid reader. At age eleven, I read James Weldon Johnson's words to "Lift Every Voice and Sing" for the first time. I understood them to be a prayer of hope. With Mother's encouragement, I learned the beautiful words of the song. Mother said they would become important during my lifetime.

In 1910, I was sent to Lane College in Jackson, Tennessee, to complete high school. At our assemblies we all sang "Lift Every Voice and Sing" and I was proud to show that I knew every word. We continued to sing "Lift Every Voice and Sing" through normal school and college. I married, became a teacher, and taught the words of "Lift Every Voice and Sing" to my students. They also proudly sang the Johnsons' song in our assemblies.

Some years later, my husband and I worked to organize a branch of the NAACP in Brownsville, Tennessee, a community in which black citizens had been denied the right to vote since Reconstruction. When we received our branch charter, the first meeting was held in our home. On that joyous date, we all stood, joined hands, and sang the words of our prayer: "Let us march on till victory is won."

These words helped sustain us during the ensuing turbulent, crisis-filled years of threats, economic reprisals, assaults, and arrests. On the night our home was completely and deliberately destroyed by fire, my husband was forced to flee. This was followed by the murder of his best friend, who, like my husband, was an officer of our NAACP branch.

On June 12, 1960, the day of my husband's death, for the first time since Reconstruction, black citizens in our hometown, Brownsville, Tennessee, stood in line before the county courthouse to register to vote—the very courthouse my husband's grandfather, a skilled brick mason, helped build and in which he had subsequently voted, during Reconstruction.

I was moved to salute my late husband that day with James Weldon Johnson's words:

*Yet with a steady beat,*
*Have not our weary feet*
*Come to the place for which our fathers sighed?*

I took my husband back to Brownsville, Tennessee, to a grove of beech trees behind the church to be buried where he had been baptized. At the gravesite where surviving NAACP members, and others, who had just registered to vote, were gathered with our family to say the last good-byes, the following words were my refrain:

*Thou who has by Thy might*
*Led us into the light.*
*Keep us forever in the path, we pray.*

And so, in December 2000, when my 105th birthday will be celebrated, I will again invoke this lyrical prayer, which will endure with me forever.

## HERB BOYD

journalist and author

When Willie Jackson moved into our neighborhood in Detroit's Black Bottom in 1951 from somewhere in Georgia, we had a ball making fun of his gold tooth and funny Southern drawl. He was the butt of our jokes, until one day he told us stories about Booker T. Washington and George Washington Carver. We thought we were pretty smart but none of us had ever heard of these great men. Jackie Robinson, Joe Louis, Jesse Owens, and Sugar Ray Robinson were the most famous black Americans in our young lives.

But Willie wasn't through. We were sitting around one afternoon reciting poetry, mostly playing the dozens, when Willie stunned us with a recitation of "Lift Every Voice and Sing." Again he had our attention, and even more so when he sang it. Without knowing it, Willie had given me my first lessons in black studies.

*Armistice Day, Lenox Avenue and West 134th Street, Harlem.* Courtesy of Schomburg Center for Research in Black Culture, The New York Public Library

I thought about Willie a lot in the late sixties, when the Johnsons' song was formally adopted in the movement as our anthem. Because of Willie, I was among the few in our circle who knew the song, though there were times when even I stumbled on the bridge, struggling to recall if it was the "faith" or the "hope" the dark past had taught us.

One of the real by-products of being introduced to "Lift Every Voice and Sing" was the discovery of James Weldon Johnson and his brother, J. Rosamond. When I began my research on them, I had no idea of their prominence in the development of the Broadway musical. Along with Will Marion Cook, Bob Cole, Ada Overton, Bert Williams, George Walker, Paul Laurence Dunbar, and Harry T. Burleigh, the Johnsons infused American popular music and the stage with a string of hit tunes and melodies, many of them poignantly laced with the best of black folklore and comedy.

At the turn of the century, even before Tin Pan Alley became the mecca of American composers, the Johnsons had a major hit song, "The Maiden with the Dreamy Eyes." This song and a passel of others were instrumental in the team signing reputedly the first exclusive contract with Stern and Marks, then one of the nation's premier publishing companies.

Further research disclosed the real Renaissance character of James Weldon Johnson, who except for W. E. B. Du Bois, Langston Hughes, Zora Neale Hurston, and Amiri Baraka is unsurpassed as a creative genius in practically every literary genre. But after all's said and done, despite *The Autobiography of an Ex-Colored Man, God's Trombones,* "Under the Bamboo Tree," and *Black Manhattan,* it's that little song written for the schoolchildren of Jacksonville, Florida, that has brought him enduring fame. And when I think of James Weldon Johnson or hear "Lift Every Voice and Sing," the memory of Willie Jackson isn't far behind.

*Tuskegee Institute faculty and board of directors posing in front of a statue of the institute's founder, Booker T. Washington, c. 1920s.* Courtesy of The Charles L. Blockson Afro-American Collection, Temple University

# EDWARD W. BROOKE

former U.S. senator, Massachusetts

I have sung "Lift Every Voice and Sing" for seventy-five years of my life. To this day, every time I sing it or hear it my eyes water and my heart beats faster. In school assemblies at Washington D.C.'s segregated John F. Cook Elementary School, Robert Gould Shaw Junior High School, and Paul Laurence Dunbar High School, I remember standing proudly with my classmates singing at the tops of our voices—first the National Anthem and then "Lift Every Voice and Sing." The two songs were intended to be inspirational as we started our school day. And they were.

The National Anthem was for all Americans, black, white, red, brown, and yellow. But "Lift Every Voice and Sing," which later became known as the Negro National Anthem, was uniquely for us. To me it spoke of black life in white America. It spoke of where we had been and where we were. It spoke of what we had learned and what we could not forget. It spoke of lingering pains of slavery and the continuing evil of segregation and discrimination. It acknowledged that progress had been made in our constant struggle for freedom but hastened to remind us that we still had a long way to go. It charged us to continue the battle for equal justice under law. It was primarily written for black children, so that they would have an awareness of the past, an understanding of the present, and hope for the future.

When I finished high school and moved on to Howard University, I continued to sing and hear "Lift Every Voice and Sing" at small and large gatherings on and off campus. The stirring words of James Weldon Johnson and the soul-gripping music of his brother J. Rosamond Johnson stayed with me when I served with the brave enlisted men and officers of the Negro 366th Infantry Combat Regiment in Italy fighting in World War II in a segregated U.S. Army to preserve world freedom and liberty. When the morale of our troops was low, as it often was, we sang our Negro National Anthem. It sustained us and helped us to carry on.

No one born black in America can really escape racism. It's in your bones. You feel it like you feel the strong human emotions of love, hate, and fear. It really never leaves your mind, your body, or your soul. You constantly pray that the feeling will go away, that things will change, that your country will live up to its promise of freedom and equal opportunity for all Americans and that black children, women, and men will be judged by their character and works, not by the color of their skin.

That's really what our great civil rights leader Martin Luther King wanted for our people. That's really what black Americans want for themselves and their children, and that's really what James Weldon Johnson and J. Rosamond Johnson wrote one hundred years ago in their musical road map for black Americans, "Lift Every Voice and Sing." They wanted us to sing it, but even more they really wanted us to live it.

## WILLIE L. BROWN, JR.

mayor, San Francisco

Like most black children who grew up in the Jim Crow South, I learned "Lift Every Voice and Sing" in my first-grade class in a segregated school. It has been an integral part of the soundtrack of my life ever since.

William Faulkner, the greatest of Southern authors, defined great writing as "creat[ing] from the raw materials of the human spirit something which did not exist before." That, it seems to me, is what James Weldon Johnson accomplished with his lyrics for what has become the "Negro National Anthem." The result is a musical poem that captures the character of a people: the strength that brought us through the long night of slavery and numbing decades of segregation and discrimination; our abiding faith and hope, despite it all; and the unique and yearning patriotism of the excluded.

There may come a time when Johnson's moving poetry will be

*"The Three Eddies," blackface entertainers, c. 1920s.* Courtesy of Schomburg Center for Research in Black Culture, The New York Public Library

seen only in the context of struggles past, but we're not there yet. Lynchings have morphed into hate crimes, which, today, earn universal condemnation. Yet the hate crimes continue, and a great question still haunts the national psyche—whether we are willing to move beyond the easy condemnation of the heinous to the hard, everyday work of eradicating racism in its more prevalent forms from the hearts and minds of the American people.

There are encouraging signs, to be sure. Our nation's growing ethnic diversity will, in time, make the struggle easier. In the meantime, however, there has been a resurgence of racist hate groups, from the lunatic fringe to such mainstream organizations as the Council of Conservative Citizens (a direct descendant of the notorious White Citizens Councils), which can count among its fans the Majority Leader of the U.S. Senate. In addition, the U.S. Supreme Court, once a critical ally in the fight for equal rights, has begun a wholesale retreat from the gains of the federal Voting Rights Act in its rush to reaffirm the tired doctrine of states' rights.

And so, one hundred years later, the struggle continues, new obstacles arise, and our anthem plays on.

## SHIRLEY CAESAR

evangelist and singer

At home, in my earliest childhood memories, the words rang out: "Lift every voice and sing. . . ." At that young age I did not know what the words meant. It did not matter. They were belted out in a manner that was foreign and lively and suggested some alternative to the more reserved nature of church. Even as a child in my choir, I understood that this hymn spoke to the very quality of life.

Composed in the ugly segregation days of 1900, James Weldon Johnson and J. Rosamond Johnson's "Lift Every Voice" speaks to the struggle of African Americans to achieve those basic freedoms we associate with happiness. For this reason, both the lyrics and the music have been humbling. They underscore that I have been

# MARCUS GARVEY

**G** Stands for Greatness,
   like our leaders of old;
**A** Stands for Ambition,
   tireless and bold.
**R** Stands for Righteousness,
   pure from within;
**V** Stands for Valor,
   striving to win.
**E** Stands for Earnestness,
   in a cause that is just
**Y** Stands for Yes,
   Negroes can win and must.

Sara R. Isaac

*"Negroes can win and must": a Marcus Garvey leaflet, 1920s.* Courtesy of The Charles L. Blockson Afro-American Collection, Temple University

# CANIBUS

rap artist

*Is the weight of your voice too heavy for you to lift?*
*How often do you work out?*
*What's the name of your gym?*
*I usually work out from 6:30 to 8 P.M.*
*4 sets of 10 reps . . . Freestyle and Free Weights*
*Neck snappin' instrumentals help me concentrate—*
*On CDs, Cassettes and Digital Audio Tapes . . .*
*Look at My Face—*
*Dark Contours, blood and sweat*
*Etched in my earthquake dreams*
*As I strain to lift two 50-pound plates*
*My larynx gets Stronger, every day that I train*
*Pumping, venting the pain of so many—*
*Forgotten—Names . . .*
*—— of KING & QUEENS.*
*I POSSESS*
*An Inner Strength . . .*
*That has nothing to do with the size of*
*My frame*
*It's an Inner Strength—*
*That can only be measured by what's inside of*
*My brain.*
*Intellect . . .*
*Has always been my favorite muscle to Flex*
*The body is controlled*
*By what is above—The Neck*
*Forever beckoning below the neck are the struggles and the*
*    stresses of the flesh*
*But the intellect Knows—below lies the depths of—*
*Hell, the Devil and Death*
*Instead, I compel you to look skyward . . . Third Eyeward*
*Reconnect the wires in your stereo deck*

*I Compel you to be one of the 144,000*
*Focus your Vocal Power AND HUHMN,*
*LIFT YOUR VOICE UP as High as the Twin Towers—*
*Don't ever allow the sound of your voice to become clouded*
*Don't ever surrender by way of the Fifth Amendment*
*If ever in doubt, remember—We are of ROYAL Descendants*
*So, exploit the First Amendment,*
*Fight for your independence,*
*Continue to Lift your Voice up!*
*They can't destroy us if we ALL*
*LIFT OUR VOICES UP—*
*—— And DEMAND RESPECT.*

# JULIUS CHAMBERS

president, North Carolina Central University

In the heat of the struggle for improved opportunities for African Americans in the 1960s and 1970s, we often turned to some unifying voice, some encouragement from our forefathers, to carry on. I frequently found that encouragement in the Negro National Anthem—"Lift Every Voice and Sing." Through the words of this song, I was reminded of the life experiences of our people during slavery and in a racially separate society. "We have come over a way that with tears has been watered." And "we have come treading our path through the blood of the slaughtered." No matter what obstacles we faced, no matter what frustration or seemingly impossible odds there were, they weren't as difficult or any more difficult than seeking freedom during slavery, or equal treatment during the era of *Dred Scott* and *Plessy v. Ferguson.*

I recall specifically the challenges that we faced during the 1960s when we sought to obtain equal accommodations and the uncertainties we felt about whether we needed to sit next to white customers. I remember our efforts to desegregate the public schools, and our concerns about whether mixing white and black

*Mr. and Mrs. James Weldon Johnson in Great Barrington, Massachusetts, 1920s.* Courtesy of The James Weldon Johnson Collection, Ollie Jewel Sims Okala, and Sondra Kathryn Wilson

students in the public schools would ultimately be in the best interest of all students and in particular whether it would be in the best interest of black students. I also recall the long hours spent trying to obtain the right to vote and to have our votes counted. At those times we needed a unifying voice, not only to push collectively for better opportunities, but also to gain some assurance that we were making the best choices in these uncharted waters. I believe, as Justice Thurgood Marshall advised us shortly before his death, that we made the best choices we could with the resources we had. I remain confident that the choices we made were consistent with those our forefathers would have made and were in the best interest of all of our people.

We face similar challenges in 2000 and we will continue to do so in the twenty-first century. Are we seeking one America, while recognizing the contributions of her diverse people? Do we achieve our objective through the affirmative, race-based measures that we have employed over the years? How do we best recognize and harness the diversity of all our people for the common good? And, more important, how do we perpetuate the resilience and motivation of our people to ensure freedom for all in this changing world? In responding to these concerns, I still like to turn to our National Anthem. There is much that is soothing and motivational in the words of the song. Words full of "faith," "hope," and "rejoicing" provide support and encouragement and the determination to move ahead, as they remind us of the struggles of our parents and how, collectively, they succeeded.

Additionally, our anthem helps us appreciate today that we have not achieved the liberty and freedom we have pursued over the years. Despite assurances from the U.S. Supreme Court and others that race no longer plays a major role in our lives, we are reminded daily by activities in this country of the continuing pervasiveness of race as a determinant of opportunity. We are also reminded that this country is much bigger and much more diverse, and that it has tremendous global influence. These developments have led some of our people to ask if the anthem itself is outdated or racist, but "Lift Every Voice and Sing" for me was written to remind all of us of the

*Jazz musician Eddie Mallory (in the light-colored suit) and the Mills Blue Rhythm Orchestra, 1933.* Courtesy of Schomburg Center for Research in Black Culture, The New York Public Library

struggles of African Americans during their history in America. Despite the changes that have occurred and that may occur in the future, we should continuously remind ourselves and all America of our history, lest the freedom and liberty that we have and that we may obtain are swept away.

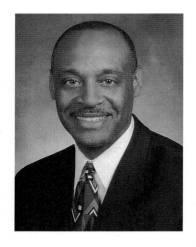

## KEVIN CHAVOUS

councilman, Washington, D.C.

There is a fitting sequel to "The Battle Hymn of the Republic." It is a song that was born from the experience of slaves. As their silken bodies struggled against the earth, as their hands and feet felt the friction of forced labor, songs of hope still poured from their mouths. Turn-of-the-century accounts recall the slaves singing, their bodies moving with hope against hope, after a full day of labor on the plantation. At night, in their small, confined quarters, they would prop their bodies up and sing until they were filled with the spirit which would propel them through another day.

Against the ruinous landscape which they helped build, hope came in the form of song. Even against the backdrop of plantation labor, their songs spoke to the eternal striving of all mankind. They spoke to a spirit that could not be destroyed, to a hope that could not be plucked from their hearts. Though enslaved by strangers, they would not destroy themselves.

Within these slave songs lies the spirit of life, the spirit of music, the spirit of God. And this spirit—faith in God and in sustaining families—was the better part of their survival. This spirit was first captured in the slave hymns and reproduced for all of us in 1900 with James Weldon Johnson's "Negro Anthem," "Lift Every Voice and Sing"—a song that ascends in our hearts because it transcends our history.

At once, "Lift Every Voice and Sing" recalls the struggle of those early African Americans who carried forth that spirit of life and reminds us that many of the fundamental freedoms we associ-

*Relaxing in front of a Harlem apartment building, 1930s.* Courtesy of Schomburg Center for Research in Black Culture, The New York Public Library

ate with happiness rest on their lofty shoulders. The lyrics and the music are humbling, insofar as they recall the selfless sacrifices of Harriet Tubman, Sojourner Truth, Frederick Douglass, Dr. Martin Luther King, Jr., and countless unknown soldiers in the fight for racial freedom and equality. I am the beneficiary of their suffering struggle, of their eternal spirit, of their spirited song, and words cannot express the depth and breadth of my gratitude.

# BILL CLINTON

president of the United States

In February 1900, brothers James Weldon Johnson and J. Rosamond Johnson stood at a special moment in time. They could look ahead to the bright promise of a new century and look behind just a generation before to a great struggle that secured the end of slavery. Out of this convergence of hope and remembrance, they wrote "Lift Every Voice and Sing," a song that vividly captures the essence of the epic journey of our nation's African Americans. Though it was written only for a small ceremony commemorating the birth of Abraham Lincoln, its powerful portrayal of anguish and of aspirations for a better life of a whole people have caused it to live well beyond that ceremony, and it has sustained millions of African Americans in the struggle for freedom and justice.

The lyrics of "Lift Every Voice and Sing" describe an unfinished journey, and, in 1900, the journey of African Americans for justice and equality was far from complete. The ensuing days, months, and years saw African Americans travel a long road toward justice, fighting laws and a society that conferred upon them second-class citizenship and institutionalized racism and oppression. "Lift Every Voice and Sing" offered guidance and inspiration in this quest, sparking African Americans to press forward until they gained access to the rights, opportunities, and experiences that long had been denied them.

*Wedding party, 1935.* Courtesy of Yvonne Benjamin

Like the Johnson brothers, we too stand at the dawn of a new century; and we too are only a generation away from a great struggle for liberty. Although we made great strides in the last century, our struggle for justice and equality for all remains unfinished. Despite an era of unprecedented prosperity, wide and disturbing disparities along color lines still exist in our nation: African Americans earn incomes that are only half those of whites; the poverty rate for African American children far exceeds that for white children; and African Americans and other minorities are far more likely to suffer from heart disease, AIDS, diabetes, and cancer. We must address these challenges if we are to become the nation we were truly meant to be. I am confident America is up to the task.

In this new century, our nation also faces an even more basic test. That challenge is for the people of our great nation to appreciate our differences while affirming our common humanity. We must find ways to respect and understand what defines each of us as individuals and not hold to the belief that our own worth increases only when someone else's is diminished. We all have the goodness within us to reach these goals, and I know that there will be a day when we achieve them. But until that day arrives our journey will not be finished, and until then, "Let us march on till victory is won."

# JOHNNIE L. COCHRAN, JR.

attorney

The words to "Lift Every Voice and Sing" were ardently spiritual for me, even in my early life. Its powerful directive is intrinsic to my roots. The significant thing about roots that have been scrupulously nurtured is that they nourish and sustain you forever, and a man who has them always knows where he stands. My own roots run through the rich black earth of my family's love, across the continent and back for better than sixty years, to a clapboard house on a red dirt hill in Shreveport, Louisiana, and to the Little Union Baptist Church.

Our pastor was Caesar Arthur Walter Clark. Reverend Clark, barely five foot five, with a mustache as neat and tiny as the man himself, never failed to deliver a riveting sermon. After his spellbinding exhortations the choir filled every corner of the church with music that sated, soothed, enlivened, and inspired. It was certainly here, in Little Union Baptist Church, that I first heard "Lift Every Voice and Sing"; its lyrics have remained with me throughout my life. I often reflect on its message: a chronicle of a people's suffering which postulates the promise of a bright future. It was this same faith in heritage, optimism, and hope expressed in "Lift Every Voice and Sing" that was bred into our close-knit family.

Early on, I believed wholeheartedly in the promise of a better future for black people in general, and the Cochran family in particular. My siblings and I were not aware of it, but we were actually poor. One of the reasons we didn't know it was our regular and lavish family dinner each Sunday. There was always fried chicken, rice, gravy, freshly baked cornbread and biscuits along with greens—mustard, turnip, or collard—macaroni and cheese, and fresh corn. Best of all, perhaps, was the dessert—deep-dish peach or apple cobbler. And, if we were lucky, my mother prepared her famous three-layer pineapple coconut cake.

Notwithstanding, the Great Depression still gripped the throats of Louisiana's working folk and Jim Crow's iron heel remained firmly planted on the necks of black men and women throughout the South. But the particular world built for us by our earnest, God-fearing, and enterprising parents, Hattie and Johnnie L. Cochran, Sr., was as secure as any palace—a home so filled with warmth, encouragement, and affection that, looking back, all that I recall is its bounty.

From our early years in rural Louisiana through our move to the urban environs of California, my father's mandate "to shine, to excel, and to take full advantage of every opportunity" has been a driving edict for me. It was, likewise, *church* and *family* that con-

*Lint Shaw, lynched by a mob near Royston, Georgia, April 28, 1936, eight hours before he was to stand trial on charges of attempted assault.* Courtesy of Schomburg Center for Research in Black Culture, The New York Public Library

joined to craft the solid foundation and approach to the intangibles of life that kept our feet "in the path" and nourished our determination to "stand . . . where the white gleam of our bright star is cast."

Every man, woman, and child in America should have the glorious opportunity to stand in a spirit-filled "Little Union Baptist Church" as the music of J. Rosamond Johnson is played for the singing of the heartfelt, inspired words of James Weldon Johnson.

# JOHNNETTA B. COLE

professor, Emory University

Each and every time I have the opportunity to lift my voice and sing our Negro National Anthem, I do so with a particular sense of connectedness that is reserved for those of us whose hometown is that of James Weldon Johnson.

To this day, I remember experiencing strong and effective antidotes to the message of second-class citizenship that the Jim Crow laws of Jacksonville, Florida, were designed to deliver to me and all African American children as we went about getting our education in that city's "colored schools." One antidote was that my teachers, beginning with Ms. Bunny Vance in the first grade, worked on the assumption that I and all of my classmates were educable; and they made sure that we came to believe in ourselves. Another powerful antidote that I consumed every day was the way my family carried itself, always saying in action and often in words that the outrageously unjust system of racial segregation would cease to be one day. And I, like everyone else of a good heart and decent soul, had a role to play in bringing it to an end.

There were also those times in my childhood when my entire being would fill with the kind of pride that challenged to its very core the notion of black inferiority. Among those experiences, I remember with particular clarity visiting Daytona Beach, Florida, to see Dr. Mary McLeod Bethune; the day Joe Louis visited Jack-

*Crowds outside the Lafayette Theatre in Harlem at the opening of the so-called "Voodoo"* Macbeth, *directed by Orson Welles and produced by the Federal Theatre Project, 1936.* Courtesy of Schomburg Center for Research in Black Culture, The New York Public Library

sonville and came to my house; going to the African American Life Insurance Company, a business my great-grandfather and six other black men had founded in 1901; hearing and watching my mother play the organ at Mount Olive A.M.E. church; and the many occasions when I joined with others in singing our Negro National Anthem.

Between those days of my childhood in the 1940s in Jacksonville, and this very day, in some ways we African American people have come so very far. And yet, how very long away seems the day when "earth and heaven ring, / Ring with the harmonies of Liberty." For if we are to know genuine liberty in this millennium, then not only must individual African Americans be able to eat at a lunch counter, but also the masses of our people must have the kind of stable and decently paid employment that makes such eating out possible. If we are to have a true democracy, then we must not only put an end to segregated schools (something we still haven't accomplished nationwide), we must also end the unequal access to technology-based information that has created the digital divide. And for African Americans who wish to pursue a college education there must be equal opportunity to do so. This nation of ours must also finally bring to a halt the inaccessibility to health services and decent housing accommodations that poverty and racism cause time and time again.

Today, at the dawn of the twenty-first century, what can we say about the hatred and the violence that continue to be perpetrated against African Americans? They must cease! How will that be accomplished? How will the liberty that James Weldon Johnson called for come about? By struggle, of course. By our continuous struggle to educate the young against racism and to vote into office those who will legislate for decent and fair opportunities. And where necessary, we must, as we did in the 1960s, agitate for what is right.

As we move now into a new millennium, let us lift our voices not only in song, but in calling for a new day for our people. And let us rededicate our energies to creating the kind of nation that James Weldon Johnson longed for and deserved.

# THOMAS COLE

president, Clark Atlanta University

Like numerous schoolchildren of my generation, I first encountered James Weldon Johnson through my reading of the collections of poetry that he penned during his career as writer and anthologist. I recall vividly the passion with which my classmates and I attempted to recite "The Creation" from *God's Trombones* in our classes or on the special occasions when orations were expected of us. Later, as a college youth, I read *The Autobiography of an Ex-Colored Man,* the pioneering African American literary classic in which Johnson examines the complex questions of race and identity in a color-conscious society. He was one of the most prolific writers of the Harlem Renaissance, and many of his artistic works found their way onto the required-reading lists of college courses in which I was enrolled. It was, however, my reading of *Along This Way,* Johnson's autobiography published in 1933, that provided the most direct insight into his life and ignited my deepest respect for and appreciation of James Weldon Johnson as educator, literary critic, distinguished poet, lyricist, diplomat, civil rights activist, and creative interpreter of the black experience.

Similarly, my earliest acquaintance with "Lift Every Voice and Sing" came on the countless occasions when my classmates and I stood proudly and sang the uplifting chords of the song popularly known as the Negro National Anthem. A soul-stirring poem set to equally soul-stirring music, this heroic song is replete with imagery of the struggles and hardships of African American life while at the same time it is deeply expressive of the hope and faith and ideals of America for all citizens. I am particularly thrilled each time I hear the lofty words and themes of this song, resonating brilliantly with honor and respect for the past, hope and encouragement for the future, conviction and belief in the promise of liberty and equality, and faith and trust in God and America.

The heroic message of "Lift Every Voice and Sing" also provides an illuminating perspective on race relations in the new millen-

*The Peace shoeshine shop, Harlem, 1930s.* Courtesy of Schomburg Center for Research in Black Culture, The New York Public Library

nium. As we sing of the faith of our fathers and mothers and of our hope for the present, we face squarely the reality that racism has not yet been exterminated and that, as we prepare for the twenty-first century, its impact is ubiquitous in our lives. Many of the complex issues of the color-conscious society that Johnson describes in his penetrating autobiography remain with us, limiting the possibilities for American achievement. "Lift Every Voice and Sing" reminds us, however, that we must believe that racial groups can live together in peace, and that we must not cease to work to achieve a society that is color blind and in which all Americans have come fully "out from the gloomy past," to stand "where the white gleam of our bright star is cast."

As we enter a new millennium, we can be emboldened further by the illuminating example James Weldon Johnson provided for all Americans with his own life and work. Johnson's inspiring message in "Lift Every Voice and Sing" is matched by his diverse and manifold contributions to culture and society in the twentieth century. His creativity and affinity for the history and popular culture of his people are immortalized in works of major import in the canon of American literature. Similarly, his ingenuity and his talent for persuading people and groups to work together for a common goal contributed significantly to the growth of the NAACP in its infancy and to reducing some of the most suffocating effects of race and inequality in American society. Johnson's reminder of hope and aspiration for the future reverberates brilliantly in each chord and stanza of "Lift Every Voice and Sing" as well as in his many other lyrics, poems, and other writings. A graduate of Atlanta University (now Clark Atlanta University), class of 1894, Johnson is by far his school's best-known alumnus, in part because of the popularity of "Lift Every Voice and Sing." I have a feeling of immense pride knowing that I serve as president of his alma mater.

# THE COTTON CLUB GIRLS

The girls of the Cotton Club Parade are more than a chorus and a line of show girls . . . they are a group of potential stars . . . any one of whom might step out tomorrow in a specialty role and stop the show. This is the type of girl selected for the Cotton Club Parade . . . the girls from whose ranks have risen such famous Sepian stars as Florence Mills, Josephine Baker, Ethel Waters and other of renown. Beauty on parade . . . yes, but more than that . . . entertainers of talent who are as important a part of the show as the stars we present.

*"Beauty on parade": The showgirls of the Cotton Club, 1930s.* Courtesy of Schomburg Center for Research in Black Culture, The New York Public Library

· 61 ·

# JOHN CONYERS, JR.

U.S. representative, Michigan

For generations of African Americans, "Lift Every Voice and Sing" has captured the essence of our struggle for life, liberty, and the pursuit of happiness in America and offered hope for a future pregnant with opportunities. "Lift Every Voice and Sing" is a serenade of struggle, perseverance, and ultimately faith. It speaks to the souls of black folk and tells the story of our first moments on the shores of America, our plight in slavery, the suffering we endured under the evil tenets of segregation and white nationalism, and our fight for equality and civil rights. Every time we sing this anthem, we are reminded of the profound magnificence of our history, our people, our strength, our potential, and, most important, our God. "Lift Every Voice and Sing" has been and continues today to serve as black America's rallying cry for attaining full citizenship without condition.

When I listen to the words so carefully crafted by James Weldon Johnson and hear the melody so beautifully scored by his brother, J. Rosamond Johnson, I think back to the first arrival of Africans in this land, in 1619. Particularly, when we lament, "Stony the road we trod, / Bitter the chastening rod, / Felt in the days when hope unborn had died," my thoughts drift to the peculiar institution of slavery. I imagine the suffering our ancestors underwent and how difficult it must have been to be enslaved in a distant land. However, I also think of the courage of Harriet Tubman, Frederick Douglass, Sojourner Truth, and William Still, who agitated for freedom long before the Civil War.

This anthem also has special significance because it evokes the civil rights movement, which is a campaign that I fully participated in, and I have continued its legacy for thirty-six years through my work in Congress. When "Lift Every Voice and Sing" invokes us to "sing a song full of the faith that the dark past has taught us, / Sing a song full of the hope that the present has brought us, / Facing the rising sun of our new day begun, / Let us march on till victory is won," I feel the dynamic energy that propelled African Americans to fight for recognition of their civil rights. It was during this period that Martin Luther King, Jr., had a dream and led a movement for inclusion of African Americans in this society. It is this same spirit that motivated me to introduce legislation making Dr. King's birthday a national holiday and to fight for its passage in Congress. Every time we sing our anthem on his birthday, I think of this critical point in history when we united as a people and with others to rally, protest, march, boycott, conduct freedom rides, and even die to end the second-class citizenship that engulfed black Americans.

Now I ask myself and you, "Why is it important for us to continue to sing this song and commemorate its hundredth anniversary, since we have overcome so much adversity?" Simply, we must continue to sing our anthem, pass it on to our children, and share it with others because it defines our history and our humanity, and it touches the human spirit. It encourages us to strive to break down the barriers of race, class, and sex that still separate all Americans.

## BILL COSBY

entertainer

There I am, singing with seventy-five light, medium, dark, and very dark brown children standing in the assembly hall. This morning, we are fresh from our apartments, fresh from being hygienically checked out by our moms and an appropriate application of Pond's Cold Cream to the ash before leaving the house for school—*fresh* from walking with books in hand, walking, talking, and hearing the merging sounds that are only found in the morning on the way to elementary school. Of course, the morning sound has its own sound, just like waking up—you walk and you don't feel so bright or happy or alert and you're arguing with the laws of some old person who says you still have to go. But the more I walk, the more I see others coming ahead of me, others behind me. The ones I like, I

*Augusta Savage at work on* Lift Every Voice and Sing, *a sixteen-foot plaster sculpture commissioned for the New York World's Fair, 1938–39.* Courtesy of Schomburg Center for Research in Black Culture, The New York Public Library

yell at, and the ones I don't—well, it's very important that they see me so that I can ig 'em (ignore them).

But wait . . . the sounds of the schoolchildren, remember? Well, the sounds at lunchtime are louder than the ones in the morning because we have to run home to eat! My mom has a bologna sandwich and canned soup for me and the radio is always on at that time, playing *Our Gal Sunday, Helen Trent,* or old *Ma Perkins.* I only know that I felt sorry for Gil Whitney 'cause he was always asking Miss Trent to marry him. . . .

Now, after eating and kissing Mom, I *run* to school—to the yard to play and work up a sweat. I scare up my school shoes and slide in on the cement. Get it? LOUD—SOUNDS—ENERGY—AWAKE! Then, the school bell! The teachers tell everyone to get in line. "Quiet, please." "Stop, please." "Don't hit, please." "Get back in place, please." "Please, please, *please.*"

Now, the three-thirty P.M. sound is almost as loud as when the war was over and the energy is way up because we're going *home!* Of course, some kids decide something has to be settled after school, and if you're lucky, you can watch it on the way home.

Anyway, I'm standing there with seventy-five kids at assembly and Miss McKinney, our teacher, was my main love. She was *dark* brown and dressed cool every day and she was cool, too. One day, after assembly, we filed into the room and she closed the door and moved to the front of her desk and started to talk to us in a way that your mother or father will tell you *not* to do something and you know that they mean it! She told us that the song we sang was *never* to be sung by her class ever again. "If they ask you to sing it, you will keep your mouth shut!" She left the room for about fifteen minutes, came back, closed the door, and proceeded to teach fractions.

I couldn't wait for assembly the next morning. I was ready to not sing that song! I was so proud of my chance to *not* sing that song. But the music director didn't ask us to sing it. Instead, we got paper with some words on it. We all knew the melody and I knew the first two sentences by heart. You see, in the Richard Allen Projects there is, or was, circa 1944, a stone sculpture of the profiles of

*J. Rosamond Johnson (foreground) leads the singing of "Lift Every Voice and Sing" at the grave of composer James A. Bland ("Carry Me Back to Old Virginny") in Bala Cynwyd, Pennsylvania, August 2, 1939.* Photograph by John W. Mosley, courtesy of The Charles L. Blockson Afro-American Collection, Temple University

three black children. All you see is the heads with open mouths singing and above them is written, "Lift Every Voice and Sing."

So, like I said, I'm standing there with seventy-five light, medium, dark, and very dark children and we are singing this morning. Miss McKinney doesn't need paper, but she starts to cry when we come to:

> *God of our weary years,*
> *God of our silent tears . . .*

I don't know why I start to cry, but whenever I get to that part of this wonderful American classic, I know that Miss McKinney moved Old Black Joe out of that assembly hall.

## Lee Daniels

editor in chief, *Opportunity* magazine

Having grown up in Boston during the early 1960s, I've always considered "Lift Every Voice and Sing" sacred music. Of all the songs sung then that blended the faith of the black church and the action of the civil rights movement, "Lift Every Voice" seemed the most serene. That was because, as I realized some years later, it is a statement, not of demonstration, but of a contemplative celebration. "Lift Every Voice" speaks not to those who would oppress us. It is our reaffirming that we remain true to what has always sustained Americans of African descent—that we remain "full of the faith that the dark past has taught us . . . full of the hope that the present has brought us."

For many African Americans, even those who are essentially agnostic, that faith and hope has always been grounded in the experience of the black church. It was no less for me; as an adolescent I drank deeply from the well of faith and compassion I found at one of Boston's most historic black churches, Twelfth Baptist Church.

There, I found all the great qualities of the Negro people expressed in their music, in songs like "Lift Every Voice."

Bernice Johnson Reagon, cofounder of the sacred-music group Sweet Honey in the Rock, once characterized African American sacred music as "music that seemed to reach inside of me and pull at feelings I didn't know I had. I felt as if I could hear my great-grandmother and great-grandfather singing." That's the way I felt then and now about "Lift Every Voice." It embodies the profound, endlessly sustaining faith of our great-grandmothers and great-grandfathers—and their great-grandmothers and great-grandfathers.

This faith and hope are a fount and a bridge. As our forefathers and foremothers used them to sustain themselves through times and circumstances much bleaker than what we face today, so we must use them to push on toward the future.

So, for me, learning "Lift Every Voice" during those wonderful years made it easy to understand that when black people sang "We Shall Overcome" they had no doubt that they would. From a people who had willed themselves to survive slavery and the era of apartheid that followed, "We shall overcome" was not a boast. It was the reality of our future.

## OSSIE DAVIS AND RUBY DEE

actors

"Lift Every Voice and Sing" is more than a song; it's also the ardent heart's barometer, used by the weary traveler to tell him where he is. We travel much each year, crisscrossing the country, on speaking engagements, public performances, lectures, rallies, demonstrations, fund-raisers, and awards ceremonies—mostly in February, which is African American History Month. Wherever we are, we always know we are home when we hear what some still call the Negro National Anthem. And that's not all we know: it's the quality of what we are hearing, the way it is sung—or not sung—that in-

*A woman carrying a bundle on her head, Natchez, Mississippi, 1930s.* Courtesy of Schomburg Center for Research in Black Culture, The New York Public Library

troduces us into the public gathering and tells us the state of the race in that environment. There are a hundred keys and tempos to which we listen—some proud, open, and defiant, some fat and satisfied, some bitter, some hesitant and quavering, just above the crying and the defeat: the singing tells us all. Then, like country doctors, we make our diagnosis, prescribing exactly what poem, or story, or folktale, or anecdotes, or lament, or flaming speech, is suitable to the occasion. Ears, too, should have a flag to wave, especially at midnight. This wonderful Song of Songs—a people's password: a bond to cinch the spirit's nationality. It always means that we are not alone.

# HOWARD DODSON

chief, Schomburg Center

I started singing "Lift Every Voice and Sing" in grade school. It was part of our morning exercises, which included a daily prayer (yes, prayer in school), the Pledge of Allegiance to the flag, and the National Anthem. In all-black John A. Watts Elementary School in "Up South" Chester, Pennsylvania, the "Negro National Anthem" formed part of the daily morning ritual that our teachers seemed to think put us in a proper frame of mind to spend the day learning.

We only sang the first verse. In all honesty, in grade school most of us never really knew the words to more than the first two lines and the triumphal "Let us march on till victory is won." Everyone chimed in on that last line, singing with great vigor as if to atone for the fact that we had mumbled our way through most of the song, lip-syncing and letting others mumble when we feared we'd be caught not knowing the song if we sang out loud. Every day for the first six years of school, my classmates and I sang the anthem. Or at least we went through the motions.

Chester is located halfway between Philadelphia and Wilmington, along the Delaware River. Though north of the infamous Mason-Dixon Line, it was in many ways during the 1940s and

*World heavyweight boxing champion Joe Louis strikes a pose, late 1930s.* Photograph by John W. Mosley, courtesy of The Charles L. Blockson Afro-American Collection, Temple University

*Mr. John Riddle, celebrating his 107th birthday, and Mrs. Riddle, surrounded by members of the Ku Klux Klan and a masked Santa Claus figure, December 22, 1948.* Courtesy of Schomburg Center for Research in Black Culture, The New York Public Library

1950s a very Southern town—"Southern" in the sense that racial segregation was very much alive and well there. The school system was racially segregated through junior high (ninth grade), so our teachers in the all-black grade and junior high schools were free to do racially specific things. Many of the unique gifts they gave us were conscious attempts to embrace and celebrate African American culture. In fact, an African American cultural ethos dominated the formal and informal activities in our all-black schools. Many of our teachers were dedicated to getting us ready for the "integration" we'd experience when we went to high school. They wanted us to be able to compete with the white folks when we enrolled in Chester High. So, they schooled us in the "classics" and other aspects of European and Euro-American culture, which were, after all, the formal, approved curriculum. But they found ways of slipping in African American stuff. Like the anthem.

I managed to get away with lip-syncing and muddling through the anthem in grade school. Not so in junior high. There, we had to learn to sing it in the choir. Ms. Louise Barnes was the music teacher and the choir director. One thing she would not tolerate was members of her choir who did not know the words to the songs. And we were also obliged to enunciate—to sing every word with the utmost of clarity. Anyone caught mumbling or lip-syncing was gone. Everyone who sang or aspired to sing wanted to be in Ms. Barnes's choir.

Ms. Barnes taught at all-black Frederick Douglass Junior High School. There was one other all-black junior high school in the city and two all-white ones. Each year, just before Christmas, there was an all-city concert. The high school choir sang. The Douglass Junior High choir sang. And a combined choir of the other black and two white junior high school choirs sang. Every year, Ms. Barnes's choir outdid them all. The other choirs sang with sheet music, presumably because they didn't know the words and the music. We rehearsed with sheet music in Ms. Barnes's choir. But we never used it in performance. And we had a very complex repertoire, ranging from Handel's *Messiah* and songs in French and Yiddish to "the anthem." We memorized every song. Every verse of every song. I fi-

*Eleanor Roosevelt poses with prominent African American Philadelphians, 1944, including Bishop David H. Sims (third from left) and contralto Marian Anderson (third from right).* Photograph by John W. Mosley, courtesy of The Charles L. Blockson Afro-American Collection, Temple University

nally learned the words to the Negro National Anthem (all three verses) in Ms. Barnes's choir.

I can't say that I really understood the meaning of those words until much later in life. Oh, the first verse was always reasonably clear. But verses two and three only began to take on real meaning for me as I probed deep and deeper into my study of African American history. Johnson obviously had a very profound knowledge of our history when he penned these verses a hundred years ago. He was, of course, one generation removed from slavery, but his proximity to that seminal period in African American history undoubtedly put him in touch with the meaning of that experience which he captured so succinctly and elegantly in those three poem/song verses. I've had to go back and study the history of slavery in order to fully appreciate the meaning of his song.

Ten years or so ago, I began reading the song as a poem. It became, for me, an ideal reading during Kwanzaa celebrations. Whenever I am asked to read something that captures the spirit of our struggle in this land, I choose one of three poem/songs—Margaret Walker's "For My People," Maya Angelou's "And Still I Rise," and James Weldon Johnson's "Lift Every Voice and Sing." When I use the anthem as a reading, I begin with the third verse (the prayer), go to the second and end with the first. This way, I am still able to end on that triumphal line, "Let us march on till victory is won." I've begun to think that maybe we should sing it that way, too!

## MELANIE K. EDWARDS

educator

For people like myself, a child of the late fifties who came of age during the radical sixties, the disco seventies, and the Me Decade eighties, "Lift Every Voice and Sing" has an impact that differs significantly from the meaning it held for persons living in the earlier decades of the twentieth century. Still, this opus is remarkable for the manner in which it acknowledges the quest and hope for a bright future eventuating from a dark and brutal past.

I was not privileged to know my gifted grandfather J. Rosamond Johnson, who passed away two years before my birth, or his brother James Weldon Johnson, who died in 1938. But I take pride in the fact that they have written a song of such strength and prophetic insight. Its spiritual impact is such that its effect is global; the song has meaning for African American people wherever they live. It is also quite exhilarating to open and peruse royalty statements, which come in from countries around the world and thus show that the hymn is still being used in public performance.

My grandfather and his brother were born six and eight years, respectively, after the end of the Civil War. The years just before and after their lives began saw congressional passage of the Thirteenth Amendment to the Constitution, the issuance of the "Black Codes" by rebel states of the Union, the ratification of the Fourteenth Amendment granting "Negroes" citizenship, passage of the Fifteenth Amendment giving us the right to vote, and the end of Reconstruction in 1876, when federal troops left the South. Against this riptide of political legislation and social change black people of all stations and classes nurtured the hope of steering their lives and the lives of their children and families toward opportunity, prosperity, and acceptance.

That the men and women of that generation could abide their subsequent disappointment and unreasonable suffering, and yet survive and cling to hope for the future, is a significant fact of that era. That duality is at the heart of "Lift Every Voice and Sing."

My peers and I, could we have marshaled our intellect, resources, and courage to fight the battles faced by J. Rosamond and James Weldon? Could we have stood against the blatant racism, the cruelty, the destruction of personhood, and the inhumanity that prevailed during their generation? Could we have found paths circumventing the racial divide and developed our minds and our talents while discharging our obligations to family and friends? Would we have been able at the same time to reach their personal, cultural, civic, intellectual, and social heights? No, I think not.

*Seeking Wisdom, 1945.* Photograph by John W. Mosley, courtesy of The Charles L. Blockson Afro-American Collection, Temple University

Our current racial, political, and societal battles are clear before us but are of a more subtle nature: Our schools are not officially segregated. Our social mobility is relatively unhampered. Our economic ceilings are present but somewhat transparent or vulnerable. Yes, we greet the new millennium with a modicum of freedom and opportunity, but we watch diligently for the next racial barrier. We are painfully aware that interpersonal and social exchange in no way equate with political and economic parity. And African Americans have not been and are not invisible in global, national, or local history as some would like to believe. I and mine have an illustrious continuity: "*I explored the Southwest with Coronado. I founded towns and banks in the Western territories. I created the precursor to the Coast Guard. I am the child of Thomas Jefferson, Senator Clay, Boston brahmins, Chief Osceola, and many slavemasters, as well as of anonymous drunken plantation overseers and traveling salesmen.*"

Our nation has far to go; by this, I am saddened. But, at the same time, I am honored that my grandfather J. Rosamond Johnson and his brother wrote a song that gives voice to the courage, faith, and hope of a people and will echo through this new century that is now begun.

# MILDRED JOHNSON EDWARDS

retired educator

At the time when I was born, "Lift Every Voice and Sing" was well into its "early adolescence." In our home the song was a living entity—you could say that it was, for me, an older sibling. My parents' friends and colleagues would seldom allow an evening of social activities or *en salon* to end without my father, J. Rosamond Johnson, playing the piano and letting them show off their harmonizing on "Lift Every Voice and Sing."

In fact, during the cultural renaissance of the 1920s and 1930s our family grew increasingly aware that the song was becoming a phenomenon. My strongest memories are of my father's obsession

*Bill "Bojangles" Robinson dances, 1940s.* Courtesy of Schomburg Center for Research in Black Culture, The New York Public Library

with and love for his music. I learned very early that he had played the piano at virtuosic levels from the age of four and had attended the New England Conservatory before relocating to the United Kingdom to complete his studies. Our home was filled with music all through the day and well into the night. My dad appreciated and played compositions by the nineteenth-century European masters but gave equal attention to his own creations. He wrote music in all styles of the period, and usually requested the opinion of his pre-pubescent daughter regarding his new tunes. Being his judge was great fun and reassured me of the depth of his love for me and his respect for my thinking.

My dad often spoke of his pleasure in the growing popularity of his song for which his brother had written lyrics. He told us of how it was being taught in black schools at all levels throughout the South and that there were also reports of its being played by symphony orchestras on the Continent. When he returned to England to continue his music studies, he was made the conductor of the Grand Opera House in London and found that his song had become widely known in music circles. He related that, whenever he entered a club over there, the house band would invariably interrupt its playing and strike up "Lift Every Voice and Sing."

During my childhood in a home filled with music, the hymn written by my father and uncle was merely one among many compositions played and enjoyed by all; however, on my own as an adult I have invoked the song's muse on innumerable occasions. During the Great Depression of the early 1930s I established a private, sleep-away summer institute, Camp Dunroven, where the song began each day for the young campers. A year later, when I founded the Modern School, a progressive experiment in secular elementary school education for local youngsters, "Lift Every Voice and Sing" was used for all official school functions and assembly. It was apparent that the song would be of great help as we strove to foster a sense of heritage and pride for the primarily African American pupils who relied on us for development and support.

"Lift Every Voice and Sing" remains for me that reliable "older sibling" in my home as well as in my life—the paradigm, the inspiration and genetic link from my family's past to posterity. May it live long after "victory is won."

## WALTER O. EVANS

surgeon

Growing up as a black child in the Jim Crow Deep South in the 1940s and 1950s, I had, if you can believe it, some advantages over my counterparts in the North. In the cities of my birth (Savannah) and my youth (Beaufort, South Carolina), black history and aspects of black culture were taught to us just as "our place in society" was infused into us. I cannot remember when I first heard "Lift Every Voice and Sing," but it most likely would have been around the same time I heard my first spiritual, gospel, or blues song. Around that same time, I would have first heard tales of Frederick Douglass, Harriet Tubman, Sojourner Truth, Paul Robeson, and other black heroes. I was introduced to the poetry of Langston Hughes, Margaret Walker, and Paul Laurence Dunbar at the same time I tasted my first savory crab or oyster. All this became an integral part of my life at a very early age. The truth is, I cannot remember ever *not* knowing "Lift Every Voice and Sing."

The town of Beaufort was steeped in antebellum and Civil War history. The city of Savannah, also steeped in history, was immortalized in James Weldon Johnson's famous funeral sermon-poem entitled "Go Down Death," which told the sad but comforting tale of Sister Caroline from Yamacraw Village. The school I first attended, the Robert Smalls School in Beaufort, had an all-black faculty and an all-black student body. Along with the basics, we were taught the history of the region. We were taught civic and personal responsibility and manners, and we were encouraged to explore and develop our own special gifts and talents. It was mandatory for each student to pursue the study of a musical instrument of his or

*Children pose for an Easter Sunday photograph, c. 1940s.* Courtesy of Yvonne Benjamin

her choice. At Robert Smalls, the teachers not only taught us, but nurtured and cared for us.

My black history lessons and nurturing came to an abrupt halt when my family moved to Hartford, Connecticut. Even though there was a sizable African American and Puerto Rican student population, the all-white Hartford High School faculty never once mentioned the contributions or accomplishments of African Americans in their curriculum. One would have thought that James Weldon Johnson had never existed and that "Lift Every Voice" had never been written! This is the same school where I quit taking saxophone lessons immediately after hearing a fellow black classmate being told by the bandleader, in front of the entire music class, that she would never be able to play the French horn because her lips were too thick. This is the same school where my counselor informed me that there was no need for me to take college prep classes, because the only jobs available to me, such as those at the Pratt & Whitney airplane engine plant, did not require a college degree.

The next time I heard "Lift Every Voice" sung was while I was attending Howard University during the civil rights era of the mid-sixties. My counterparts from the North thought that this "new" song had been created solely for the movement. Needless to say, they were amazed that I had learned the words and melody so quickly!

Now, of course, this wonderfully uplifting song is an American tradition and is sung and accepted throughout the *entire* nation, as it should be . . . as it should always have been.

*Jazz musician Louis Armstrong signs autographs for young admirers, 1940s.* Photograph by John W. Mosley, courtesy of The Charles L. Blockson Afro-American Collection, Temple University

# Myrlie Evers-Williams

civil rights leader and author

The history of our people began with a song.

Whether in times of celebration or in times of sadness, music was in the soul of Africa, and in the souls of her people. Rhythmic drums beat out harmonious messages that heralded with joy the birth of a new arrival or resonated with sorrow at the death of a king. Poetry and prayers set to music found their way across the wide divide of oceans and continents, stowed away in the hearts of our African ancestors who huddled in the narrow bellies of slave ships. The songs lay dormant in their hearts until awakened in the cotton fields of Southern plantations and in the factories and migrant towns of the North. Spirituals and folk songs wailed across the majestic purple plains of America, denouncing the pain of slavery or silently whispering prayers for angelic deliverance.

One can only imagine the surge of emotions experienced by James Weldon Johnson as he penned the song "Lift Every Voice and Sing" in 1900. He must have visualized an oppressed people who had traveled far, but not far enough; who were weary but "no ways tired"; who were free in spirit, but shackled by the chains of slavery.

I, too, have become filled with the tears of my ancestors as we sing, "Facing the rising sun of our new day begun, / Let us march on till victory is won." This emblematic phrase has special meaning to me, as it exemplifies the kinetic spirit of the 1996 national convention of the National Association for the Advancement of Colored People. Indeed, the theme that year, "A New Day Begun," was taken from "Lift Every Voice." Although the song had long been an inspirational anthem at African American gatherings, it had also become a soothing mantra to refresh my battle-weary spirit whenever faced with one more incident of racism, one more campaign against segregation. It was particularly fulfilling for me during that time to join with all those passionate voices melodiously singing in celebration of the rebirth of the NAACP.

"Lift Every Voice" raises awareness of self . . . of the historic coming of age of a mighty and powerful race of people. But the words, the heartfelt meaning, and the historical value of the song seem foreign to our young people. How ironic that one hundred years ago, five hundred children first sang "Lift Every Voice" during a birthday tribute to President Abraham Lincoln. Now, at the dawn of a new century, our children remain somehow oblivious, even somewhat impassive, about their history. But they must know, and we must teach them.

The future of our people begins with a song, and it will be the voices of our children that will sing it.

*Reena Evers-Everette, Darrell Evers, Myrlie Evers-Williams, and Van Evers*

# REENA EVERS-EVERETTE

business executive

# DARRELL EVERS

photographer

# VAN EVERS

artist

"Lift Every Voice and Sing" is a musical masterpiece with lyrics that inspire strength, determination, sacrifice, hope, and faith in God. Just thinking about the song brings forth powerful memories of historical events of the past that flow into today's realities.

In our early life in Jackson, Mississippi, the Negro National Anthem was sung at every public event: church services, school programs, mass meetings, and street demonstrations. The song emerged to greater heights during the modern civil rights movement of the 1960s.

We, the Evers children, were required to know the melody and all three stanzas of "Lift Every Voice and Sing" as small children.

*An evening of fun and dancing at the USO, 1940s.* Photograph by John W. Mosley, courtesy of The Charles L. Blockson Afro-American Collection, Temple University

Our parents, Medgar Wiley Evers, NAACP field director, and Myrlie Evers, insisted that we know and understand the song as part of our awareness of history, to instill pride in us about our heritage, and to make us stronger individuals.

Our mother was a classical pianist, so music was woven into the fabric of our lives. Many of our enjoyable family moments were spent gathered around the piano singing. Of course, "Lift Every Voice and Sing" was always an Evers family favorite.

We recall so vividly the nightly mass meetings where hundreds, sometimes thousands of people gathered in churches or at the Masonic Temple on Lynch Street in Jackson. We heard speeches by such greats as Thurgood Marshall, Lena Horne, James Baldwin, Dick Gregory, Roy Wilkins, and local freedom fighters. Their speeches never failed to inspire us to continue to fight for a better day. "Lift Every Voice" was usually sung at the beginning of these events, and each word was sung with poignant meaning and determination. Often these programs ended with the song "We Shall Overcome." Everyone left with a renewed spirit and an even greater commitment to the struggle for civil rights.

Although many positive changes have taken place in civil rights in this nation, we cannot rest on our laurels. We cannot allow the descendants of our forefathers to forget the gruesome truth—the consequences of racial injustices. We must not forget the momentous price paid, and the fortitude to fight on that is found only in the acknowledgment that our strength comes from our God, Who inspired James Weldon Johnson to write our song of freedom. This historical point must be instilled in our children. The words to "Lift Every Voice and Sing" must remain alive in our memories and our hearts until the battle for equality is won, and thereafter.

# JOHN HOPE FRANKLIN

historian, Duke University

My mother was not a pianist, but she sang beautifully without accompaniment. As she did her chores about the house, she sang and hummed tunes. It was at such a time that I first heard "Lift Every Voice and Sing." I must have been six or seven years old. When we moved from Rentiesville, Oklahoma, to Tulsa in 1925, the song took on an exciting new meaning. At Booker T. Washington High School, which I attended from the seventh grade until graduation, we had assembly twice each week. Two things stand out during those years. One was the favorite admonition of Ellis W. Woods, the principal, who stood in the halls and told the students to keep to the right and keep going. The other was the manner in which Mrs. Carrie Booker Person, the director of music, hit the chords on the piano at the end of assembly. It was the signal for us to stand up and sing "Lift Every Voice and Sing." There was nothing military about the anthem, but Mrs. Person played it with spirit, and we sang it with as much spirit as the Marines or the Army put into their songs. During those years, I learned the words to James Weldon Johnson's masterpiece and began to understand what they meant.

It was when I was a student at Fisk University that "Lift Every Voice and Sing" became a part of me. At that time, James Weldon Johnson was the Adam K. Spence Professor of Creative Literature, and we students actually had the opportunity to meet him and, if we desired, to work with him. He was working on his autobiography, which would soon be published as *Along This Way*. During one of those years—1933, I believe—Johnson gave a series of lectures called "Life, Art, and Letters," much of which material appeared in the autobiography. One day, in the course of his lecture, he recited "Lift Every Voice and Sing," and for the first time I was able to ponder the words and savor their meaning. Whenever I hear the words today, I can hear James Weldon Johnson admonishing me to keep the faith, "true to our God / true to our native land." And I try very hard to do just that.

*Members of the Elks greet one another at a convention, 1940s.* Photograph by John W. Mosley, courtesy of The Charles L. Blockson Afro-American Collection, Temple University

# Elizabeth Garlington

retired social worker

"Lift Every Voice and Sing," and its author, James Weldon Johnson, had an impact on me early on and this amazing song has continued to be a powerful force in my life. I met Mr. Johnson during the late 1920s when I was a very young student from Abbeville, South Carolina, at the Atlanta University Laboratory School. Johnson was a university alumnus and he would visit our college campus about twice a year to talk to the student body. I recall being quite impressed with him and his song. He was an inspiration and I was in awe! His own life seemed to embody the school motto, "Find a way or make one." Out of all of our struggles and hardships, to find a way to come up with a song like that is quite amazing. The sentiments of Johnson's song and our school motto helped guide me through three graduations at Atlanta University and long afterward. I completed the Laboratory School in the spring of 1928 and joined Atlanta University's last undergraduate class, graduating in June 1932. My third Atlanta University graduation was in 1934 from the School of Social Work. The spirit of "Lift Every Voice and Sing" came with me to St. Louis, Missouri, where I was a pioneer in the social work field as the first black social worker at the Red Cross and helped in opening the schools of social work in my adopted city to black graduate students.

"Lift Every Voice and Sing" conjures up many thoughts and feelings in me. It has given me a sense of pride and a sense of who I am as a black person. It contains the full spectrum of human emotions in a strong, melodious message. Its combination of words, melody, and rhythm seldom fail to work like magic when problems and demands seem overwhelming. But most of all, it elicits a strong statement of the struggle of Africans in the Diaspora. I have carried that sense of pride into my almost seventy years of work as a social worker, NAACP activist, church leader, and strong community advocate.

The song evokes a spiritual mood, like a prayer. If I'm sad when

I hear it, it lifts me. We have this song as a source of solace. So great feelings of pride well up in me and I begin to notice how happy we all are when we sing it. I feel emotional, especially when it gets to the lyrics: "God of our weary years, God of our silent tears." This is where it brings back some unpleasant memories. Certain experiences of racism are difficult to get over, even after living more than ninety years.

Before this magnificent song, we sang songs like "John Brown's Body" or "The Battle Hymn of the Republic." These were abolitionist songs. But "Lift Every Voice and Sing" was by a black person. It was written out of the experiences and hardships of black people and it's a beautiful song because it raises our hopes and dreams.

While I've been angry about second-class citizenship and being denied privileges, I am pleased with being black and being in the struggle. The song speaks to this; it tells us to rejoice but it also speaks of strength and perseverance and reassurance. It is indicative of our culture as we have stood up and fought back even though we have been knocked down. In spite of that, we knew there was a brighter day and we could overcome and endure. So it is our bright and morning star.

Singing means a lot to me, it is like the balm of Gilead, an elixir, so to speak. And while I don't consider myself a singer, I can sing three songs well: "Happy Birthday," the Lord's Prayer, and "Lift Every Voice and Sing."

## NIKKI GIOVANNI

poet and scholar

This is the way I heard the story. My family is from Albany, Georgia—my mother's family, that is. My father's family is from right outside Mobile, Alabama, and they don't figure in this. My great-grandmother Cornelia Watson, for whom I am named, had a daughter whom my mother and her sisters called Aunt Daughter.

*A young boy rests on his plow, King and Anderson Plantation, near Clarksdale, Mississippi, 1940.* Courtesy of Schomburg Center for Research in Black Culture, The New York Public Library

Aunt Daughter, who may have been named Agnes or Elizabeth, was being courted by a young man in Jacksonville. The family was not pleased, as the Watsons had worked hard to accumulate land and they were landowners and businessmen. (My grandfather John Brown Watson, named for the true great emancipator, was allowed to attend Fisk University because he was considered a bit of a dreamer. The family, in fact, called him "Book," and though he was wiry and strong like his mother, he seemed to lack the killer instinct of his father's family.) Aunt Daughter was quite taken by the young man from Jacksonville, and she asked her younger brother, John, to intercede with the family for permission to marry. Everyone considered John Brown a level-headed young man, what with him having graduated from Fisk University and not Tuskegee or an A&M, so when he suggested that his mother, Cornelia, whom we called Mama Dear, and Aunt Daughter travel to Jacksonville to meet the young man's family, everyone thought that was a fine idea. John Brown agreed to chaperone the two women, though his wife was not pleased.

The young man's family was pleased to welcome the "Georgia Delegation." They were, in fact, educated, cultivated people who were as picky about their son as the Watsons were their daughter. They planned a big gathering for the visitors, with many friends and acquaintances of the young man and his family in attendance. The young man and his brother provided the entertainment. They sang a wonderful song about being "wild about Harry," whoever Harry was, and though it was a fun song there seemed to be a bit of . . . well . . . undertow. The young man and his brother were talking about "shufflin' along" when they got to New York, but my great-grandmother did not believe Negroes should shuffle and she didn't care at all for her baby going up to Harlem with all that wild night-life. Mama Dear put her back up, but Aunt Daughter was evidently so taken (and John Brown seemed to be approving) that she let it slide.

When the company left, the family sat down to late supper. The young man's mother said: "James, why don't you lead us in thanksgiving for this company and this meal?" And James bowed his head

*Jazz pianist and bandleader Earl "Fatha" Hines (left) jams with Thomas Wright "Fats" Waller in 1942.* Photograph by John W. Mosley, courtesy of The Charles L. Blockson Afro-American Collection, Temple University

and, having noted the disapproval of Mama Dear earlier, said: "Lift every voice and sing, till earth and heaven ring. Ring with the harmonies of liberty. Let our rejoicing rise high as the listening skies. Let it resound loud as the rolling seas. Amen." Mama Dear noted that that was a very fine prayer, but she couldn't help but say that this is not what she had in mind for her baby, and she, not wanting to waste the Johnsons' time, hopes everyone understands why she cannot approve of this marriage. James was crushed. And so was Aunt Daughter, who went on to marry a preacher and live in Baltimore. But James's brother, Rosamond, convinced him to travel to New York, where they would, in fact, do very well. Everyone remembered that lovely prayer, and the family would periodically ask James to say it. Rosamond thought it would be a mighty pretty song. But it wasn't until James became a big fan of the Negro Baseball League that he could allow himself to once again embrace that difficult time of his first love. He was in the stands one afternoon when "The Star-Spangled Banner" was sung and he said: "We should have our own anthem." He and Rosamond went home and that evening took that little prayer and added: "Sing a song full of the faith that the dark past has taught us. Sing a song full of the hope that the present has brought us." And when they got to that line, Rosamond knew that his brother was coming out of his blues for Aunt Daughter and would find true love again. Rosamond suggested: "Facing the rising sun of our new day begun, let us march on till victory is won. *Play ball.*"

And that's the story I was told.

[Editors' note: Nikki Giovanni's charming folktale represents a fanciful version of how the "anthem" label of "Lift Every Voice and Sing" evolved.]

*Day laborers chopping cotton, Hopson Plantation, Clarksdale, Mississippi, 1940.* Courtesy of Schomburg Center for Research in Black Culture, The New York Public Library

# OSCAR GOMEZ

executive, GTE Sprint

"Lift Every Voice and Sing" is a heavenly horn, calling forth in each of us a renewed and higher purpose that benefits mankind. It is a hymn of faith, hope, and love—of our country and our God. Even in the midst of great trouble, God's blessings have been like sunlight to growing flowers . . . flowers planted along a stony road. That's why it's important not to forget the suffering. Suffering is heavy. At times, life hurts so intensely and with such force that we scream in terror or cry out with pain. But the intensity of our suffering does not compare to the glory that comes through faith . . . and progress.

"Lift Every Voice and Sing" floods each crevice of the heart, embracing the power, passion, and pain of struggle and yet the gentleness of living by the Spirit. Francis de Sales once said, "Nothing is so strong as gentleness; nothing so gentle as real strength." Life is like a powerful current; we can go with it or against it. To row a boat upstream is a constant, excruciating battle, and to rest, for even a brief moment, is to move back farther than the distance gained on the previous stroke. In this context, life is a battle, and we are always but a short step from difficulty. However, move with the current and we find almost superhuman strength. This beautiful hymn, these prayerlike words, are just as meaningful now as they were when James Weldon Johnson wrote them so many years ago. He reminds us even today that we have a stake in shaping the world—in our city, in our community, on our street.

As we continue to travel life's stony road, let us not forget those who walked in the dark past without light. Let us not forget those who shed blood and died so that we could stand erect. And let us not forget about the journey ahead—until victory is won for all citizens, and every voice can sing.

# Jeanne Belle Osby Goodwin

retired educator

*Stony the road we trod,*
*Bitter the chastening rod,*
*Felt in the days when hope unborn had died;*
*Yet with a steady beat,*
*Have not our weary feet*
*Come to the place for which our fathers sighed?*

I can't remember where or when I first heard the Negro National Anthem. Possibly at the Culture Club meetings at the Union Baptist Church in Springfield, Illinois, where I was born (July 6, 1903) and bred.

In Springfield we were a diverse collection from everywhere. Many of my classmates from first grade through high school were first-generation Americans whose parents had come from "the old country"—Ireland, Germany, Italy . . .

I attended integrated schools with no black teachers until I entered Fisk University (1921). But I was born to a typical Negro family. My paternal grandmother was the child of an African slave woman and her master. My maternal grandfather was a Brewington originally from Tennessee; he had migrated from Illinois to Haiti hoping to escape slavery, only to find living conditions there unbearable. They returned my great-grandfather (Henry Brewington) to the United States of America by way of Ohio. There my grandfather met and married an Irish girl. They came on back to Litchfield, Illinois, where they resettled on Butternut Grove farm.

It was to Butternut Grove my mother took us in July 1909 to escape possible harm from the rioting in Springfield. Fortunately, we lived across town (only two miles from Abraham Lincoln's tomb in Oak Ridge cemetery), but my father was afraid the bloodshed might spread. We stayed out of town three or four days.

Though my parents' education was limited, we were encouraged to be the best we could possibly be at school and church. My

*Nightclub scene, late 1940s.* Courtesy of Schomburg Center for Research in Black Culture, The New York Public Library

father said, "Clothes wear out; money is spent—but if you get knowledge it will stay with you."

The NAACP was organized (Mary Church Terrell in New York and Dr. W. E. B. Du Bois and the Niagara Movement) following the riot at home in 1909.

Although we were the only "blacks" in our classes usually, our parents were happy to have my sister Mayme, my niece Jewel, and me receive the gold medal for proficiency in American history given annually to sixth-graders by the D.A.R. (Daughters of the American Revolution) at Enos School.

We couldn't afford a car but we grew up owning the Harvard Classics. I still have some volumes. Baptists-Republicans, we lived the essence of the Negro National Anthem, and certainly sang it with great appreciation at Fisk University, where W. E. B. Du Bois was a trustee and his daughter, Yolande, a classmate. At ninety-six, I still sing

> *Keep us forever in the path, we pray.*
> *Lest our feet stray from the places, our God, where we met Thee,*
> *Lest our hearts, drunk with the wine of the world, we forget*
>     *Thee.*

# AL GORE, JR.

vice president of the United States

One hundred years ago, when James Weldon Johnson wrote the words to "Lift Every Voice and Sing," he could not have imagined the struggle and salvation, the pain and progress, of the ensuing century.

Because of the leadership of people like W. E. B. Du Bois, Martin Luther King, Jr., and James Weldon Johnson himself—and because of the boundless courage of thousands of Americans of all races—this century has been one in which we have expanded the promise of America to millions of our brothers and sisters.

My commitment to the civil rights struggle is a deeply personal one. I watched my father, when he was a U.S. senator from Tennessee, take courageous stands for civil rights. He opposed the poll tax in the 1940s, supported civil rights in the 1950s and voting rights in the 1960s, and was one of only three southern senators to refuse to sign the hateful Southern Manifesto opposing integration in our schools. He lost his Senate seat because of his stands, but his conscience won. And he taught me that that was what really counted.

I believe that the progress we have made in civil rights in the twentieth century must be only the beginning of the progress we will make in the twenty-first. We need to open up the doors of opportunity—through affirmative action and a vigorous enforcement of the civil rights laws. We need to rejuvenate communities that have been neglected for too long, by creating empowerment zones to attract jobs and spur growth. And we must make sure that all our children have the skills to seize the jobs of the future. That is why we have to bring revolutionary improvements to our public schools.

We are a great nation not in spite of our diversity, but because of it. The struggle that has drawn so much inspiration from James Weldon Johnson's words is not over until all Americans are welcomed into our national community—until every voice can be lifted together in song. At the dawn of this new century, let us sing with added purpose Johnson's familiar verse: "Facing the rising sun of our new day begun, let us march on till victory is won."

# EARL GRAVES

president and CEO, *Black Enterprise* magazine

James Weldon Johnson's sobering and passionate "Lift Every Voice and Sing" is more than just a song. It is an exhortation, a guiding spirit that symbolizes a people's valiant past and goals yet to be accomplished. It has helped to give me direction throughout my life.

*Students in front of Frederick Douglass Memorial Hall, Howard University, Washington, D.C., 1940s.* Courtesy of Schomburg Center for Research in Black Culture, The New York Public Library

I first became acquainted with "Lift Every Voice and Sing" at St. Philip's Episcopal Church in Brooklyn's Bedford-Stuyvesant section, a predominantly black community. Sundays were "wake up, get dressed for church" days for my brother, my two sisters, and me. At first, I didn't fully understand the meaning and significance of the lyrics. As I stood at my parents' side, I listened as they and other worshippers sang, often while holding hands in a communal bond.

As time went on—from childhood to adulthood—from college to the U.S. Army; from aide to Senator Robert F. Kennedy to publisher of *Black Enterprise* magazine—I began to understand why the song invoked such reverence, and why it is often referred to as the Negro National Anthem.

"Lift Every Voice" has helped me find and define my voice—that is, my role as a proud black man; as a husband, as a father, and as a businessman. "Sing a song full of the faith that the dark past has taught us, / Sing a song full of the hope that the present has brought us": Those words affirm that we are the living embodiment of a vibrant, resilient people.

"We have come over a way that with tears has been watered, / We have come treading our path through the blood of the slaughtered": Those words, focusing us as a people, graphically remind us of those who lifted their voices and even sacrificed their lives to achieve the gains we have made. But while individual achievement is admirable, it is through collective action and leveraging our purchasing and investment power that we will achieve equality, wealth, and independence.

I still sing "Lift Every Voice" when I meet with civil rights groups. I hear the words emanating joyously from student choruses at historically black colleges. And I sing it with men and women in Greek letter organizations and community groups. We still hold hands, in an affirmation of our shared heritage and goals. And for those who don't know the words, find a way to listen to them, and the spirit will come to you, as it came to me. And together, as Mr. Johnson urged, "Let us march on till victory is won."

# C. BOYDEN GRAY

former White House counsel (Bush administration)

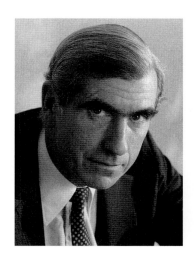

As I reflect on "Lift Every Voice and Sing," I recall the struggle of black Americans to achieve those fundamental rights we associate with freedom. As we now stand on the doorstep of a new millennium, we are presented with an opportunity to pay homage to their struggle. They were our torchbearers in the dark, propelling us forward with the singular knowledge that there is no biological difference between a black boy and a white boy. In other words, there is nothing innately black or white about either of these human beings.

Yet, as a white man born into privilege in this country, I am well aware of the advantages white males have here. The not so subtle ways in which advantages develop dates back to the days of slavery. That is to say, the differences of today aren't as much about skin color as about cultural patterns that slavery wrought. It is about cultural division that was sewn so deeply into our social fabric, for so long, that even today we have trouble imagining ourselves as the "other" skin color.

Many of those who live in suburban enclaves, aware of having come out on the privileged side of these social divisions, go to great pains to keep the mysterious and inferior "others" out. They protect their social roles by vigorously proclaiming that blacks score lower on aptitude tests. They maintain that blacks have not achieved the same manner of success as whites in the arts and sciences. It does not occur to them that even though blacks have historically been denied equal opportunity, adequate role models, or even the equal expectation of success, they have made important contributions to many aspects of our culture without which our country would be unrecognizable. If blacks have failed to match whites in the sheer breadth of their social endeavors, a lot of the gap is the result of habit and tradition.

I have fought in my everyday life, through example, to change this. As someone who was counsel to Vice President and President

*Woman day laborer chopping cotton, Knowlton Planta‡ion, Pethshire, Mississippi, 1940.* Courtesy of Schomburg Center for Research in Black Culture, The New York Public Library

Bush for twelve years, I have had the opportunity to sit at the pinnacle of power. I do understand that there are advantages that go along with being born white in America. And those advantages must be extended so that they are viewed not just as black or white advantages, but as human ones. As we enter the new millennium, we must lift all voices regardless of race, creed, or background and sing together as a wondrous human chorus.

Recently, social roles have become less rigid, allowing more and more who were denied opportunities to pursue the human endeavor that best suits their individual merit, rather than one dictated by the pigmentation of their skin. Still, racial injustices linger, and even one racial injustice is far too many. Perhaps by better celebrating the great gift of our past and giving credit where credit is due, we can propel ourselves forward into a thousand years of social harmony. This is the most important key to unlocking this country's potential in the new millennium.

# WILLIAM H. GRAY III

president and CEO, United Negro College Fund

As long as I can remember, "Lift Every Voice and Sing" has been *our* song.

One of the few benefits of growing up in the South was that each day in school, we slowly and majestically sang this melodious anthem that was created by one of our poets—a song that promises us that if we keep struggling, we will see the light of freedom because of our faith.

We all know that segregation in America was a great injustice. And having grown up when and where we did, those of my generation—people who have experienced Jim Crow—can reflect on a few things that helped to strengthen and sustain us during that sad period. And "Lift Every Voice and Sing" is one of them.

Just think, at the start of each school day during those turbulent times, we sang *our* song; it is ironic that nowhere in James Wel-

*Langston Hughes (standing) at a reception in his honor, 1943.* Photograph by John W. Mosley, courtesy of The Charles L. Blockson Afro-American Collection, Temple University

don Johnson's anthem is the word "race" mentioned. The issue of color is never even hinted at. But the message, in words and phrases so full of allegory and imagery, is so clear that you cannot sing or even read the lyrics without getting the feeling that despite how hard they are, things will get better—a brighter day is coming.

"Lift Every Voice and Sing" may have been written a hundred years ago, but there are times when it feels as though it were written just yesterday. The words still speak to the experience of the African American struggle. The words "bitter the chastening rod, / Felt in the days when hope unborn had died" have just as much meaning in 2000 as they did in 1900.

On another level, I must admit to personal satisfaction when I help today's children grasp the full meaning of *our* song. As a minister, I have had more than a couple of occasions to enlighten children who seem to be singing it as just another song. Once you start teaching it to them, going over it line by line, you can see the children grow inside and then, suddenly, their eyes light up and they get it. They clearly understand the meaning. That is when a surge of hope wells up inside and you realize that James Weldon Johnson made an indelible impression upon our souls. He did a better job than he realized. And we cannot help but swell with pride when we realize that "Lift Every Voice and Sing" is, and always will be, *our* song.

## JACK GREENBERG

former director, NAACP Legal Defense Fund

As I thought of the impact on me of "Lift Every Voice and Sing," I reflected on my emotional response to certain music. "The Star-Spangled Banner" gives me goose bumps. I have been told that it is musically not very good, being extremely difficult to sing, and that it exalts warfare and violence. But, as I listen and sing, I don't make a calculated judgment, I just feel a slight shiver. Every five or ten years, usually on an airplane, I see the movie *Casablanca*. There is a scene in which a Nazi platoon invades Rick's bar in Casablanca in search of a spy. As the soldiers arrogantly abuse the diners and drinkers seated around the dining room, they stand spontaneously and defiantly sing the "Marseillaise," humiliating the intruders. When I see this I cry. And I try to fight back tears when seeing or hearing Beethoven's *Fidelio,* as the prisoners, clad in rags, limping and crawling, emerge from their dungeon into the light and freedom. This scene is so powerful a testament against tyranny that its performance was prohibited in the Soviet Union during the reign of communism.

I cannot count the times I have stood in a group committed to the struggle for equality and sung "Lift Every Voice and Sing"—in churches, at meetings, sometimes, unhappily, at funerals. As I traveled across the country during the years I tried civil rights cases and directed the NAACP Legal Defense Fund, I got that same tingling feeling when I heard it. And I still do. Like the other music I have described, it expresses a yearning for freedom and envelops the listener in a feeling of community. It proclaims the unity of those of us who were "march[ing] on till victory is won." And, it foretells a time when, like the prisoners who crawl to the light in *Fidelio,* those who suffered the "chastening rod" will stand in the "white gleam of our bright star." The dark rhythmical passages, accompanied by a steady beat at a low pitch, depict "the days when hope unborn had died." But soon we come to soaring melodic lines that take us "out from the gloomy past." It is an emotional roller coaster that leaves us full of hope and primed to engage in the struggle for freedom.

*Members of the Negro League New York Cubans in the dugout, c. 1940s.* Photograph by John W. Mosley, courtesy of The Charles

L. Blockson Afro-American Collection, Temple University

# Lani Guinier

law professor, Harvard University

"Uprising from a Downfall," an elderly black woman at a bookstore in Philadelphia proposed to name the book I was then writing about my experience coping with a public disappointment, the withdrawal in 1993, without a Senate confirmation hearing, of my nomination to head the U.S. Justice Department's Civil Rights Division. In my public humiliation she saw the human cost of a competitive political culture in which everything is zero sum: my gain is inevitably your loss. I should use the opportunity, she said, the opportunity of getting right back up, to speak my mind, tell the truth, stand up to power, honor my principles. "You spoke truth to power," she announced, her voice much stronger than her lean, frail body. "You refused to back down, and now, you have inspired others to lift themselves up too." She leaned closer to me from across the table where I was signing the book of law review articles that had gotten me into so much trouble. "Every time God closes a window, He opens a door," she told me.

In my willingness to fight back she found a lesson of redemption from betrayal: the betrayal, as Christopher Lasch has observed in other contexts, is the betrayal of American democracy by America's political elites; the redemption, as Cornel West reminds us, is in the heroic energy of the men and women whose commitment to meaningful, down-at-the-grassroots democracy makes everything else possible. By speaking out I might inspire more people to join me in the public square. By fighting back, I might inspire others, too, to struggle to redeem their democracy.

It was the experience of not being able to speak for myself during the nomination debacle that taught me important lessons about how the civil rights movement itself has been silenced and how we need to reconnect to the true source of our voices in order to be heard once again. I learned that when we struggle with others we gain a sense of our own power to resist injustice and to make things better for more than only ourselves.

*Paul Robeson, 1940s.* Photograph by John W. Mosley, courtesy of The Charles L. Blockson Afro-American Collection, Temple University

If we succeed it will be because ordinary Americans join together, moved by a new vision of social justice that they themselves have made. I believe that can happen, but only if we lift every voice.

No one could say it better than the words of the African American National Anthem: we can create our own future, full of the faith that the dark past has taught us. If we raise our voices in unison, we shall reclaim our own very real power. Earth and heaven shall ring. Our rejoicing shall rise high as the listening skies, and resound loud as the rolling sea. I had no choice, it now seems. I named my political memoir *Lift Every Voice*.

## LOUIS HARRIS

pollster and civil rights activist

At the age of six I was enrolled in the Worthington Hooker School in the well-to-do Whitney Avenue–Prospect Street section of New Haven, Connecticut. One of my closest friends was Sam McCracken, who was black, the son of a janitor in an apartment building in the neighborhood. One day in class, we read the book *Little Black Sambo,* which was standard classroom fare in 1927. I noticed during the reading that Sam seemed to get increasingly upset. He seemed to slump and bury his head till the end of school. After school, I sensed something was awry, and we walked home together. Halfway home, Sam broke up into uncontrolled sobbing. The story of Black Sambo was just too much for him to endure. Somewhere in me, some voice told me that an injustice had been done. I hugged Sam and tried to give him solace. Our friendship was bonded deeply after that. He was the only black in the class and felt he had been singled out cruelly. This episode stuck in my memory for the rest of my life.

I had an uncle I was close to who had gone to Yale. When it came time for me to go to college, he suggested that I go to school not in my hometown but in another part of the country. He recommended the University of North Carolina at Chapel Hill. It was a

*Holding class in a one-room schoolhouse, Mileston Plantation, Mississippi, c. 1940.* Courtesy of Schomburg Center for Research in Black Culture, The New York Public Library

choice that would change my life. There, I became a student leader and I acquired my role models. Dr. Frank Porter Graham was the president of the university. Although the university had no black students, Dr. Frank, as we called him, made no bones about his deep feelings about racial equality. I wrote many editorials in the *Daily Tar Heel* about the need for the university to enroll black students. In the summer of 1941, Dr. Graham recommended me to a summer leadership institute on Campobello Island, the home of President and Mrs. Roosevelt. I attended that institute and there acquired my second role model, Mrs. Roosevelt. I quickly found that she felt as deeply as Dr. Frank and I on matters of race. One evening in a conversation, when I asked her why she was so active on the subject of race, she replied, "We cannot feel we have the equality guaranteed in our Constitution and our Bill of Rights as long as one-tenth of our population languishes behind the rest only because of their race. I have access to the President, and feel compelled to press my case of this basic issue over and over again."

In 1942 I organized a major protest rally, which attracted more than eight hundred supporters, demanding that blacks be admitted to the graduate school. I always felt that college was a time of trial and error to test out what you might do for the rest of your adult life. It was there in Chapel Hill that I took a deep resolve that working for racial quality would be a major commitment in my life. It has been a vital part of my personal life, especially when my daughter married a black lawyer, a marriage that sadly didn't last, but affected all our lives and sensibilities. I still don't know what it is like to be discriminated against solely because of the color of your skin. But I have come close.

Without question, the great disgrace of America is our systematic and pervasive insistence on disabling African Americans on the basis of their race. I fight it every day of my life. I remember the unkind cut to my friend Sam McCracken. "Lift Every Voice and Sing" inspires me all the more in this mission.

# DOROTHY I. HEIGHT

president emeritus, National Council of Negro Women

I first learned and recited "Lift Every Voice and Sing" as a poem written by James Weldon Johnson. I was a member of the Harlem Christian Youth Council when the sheet music was presented. We were inspired with its wonderful melody. We read it aloud together, then shared our sense of its meaning. Once we sang it, it became our own. We sang the third stanza prayerfully, feeling one another's sense of struggle and hope. To this day, I find it hard to sing just one stanza. The words and melody linger on.

I have seen firsthand the impact of the song in many different contexts throughout the years. I find it a trusted leadership tool. It stimulates unity. It motivates. In my training of volunteers and staff for the YWCA of the USA, women of all races from all parts of the country and many parts of the world taught me the universal appeal of this song in all the ways they responded. It became a rallying point as the YWCA adapted its One Imperative for the elimination of racism wherever it exists and by any means necessary. "Lift Every Voice" is a great carrier of values and of history.

My appreciation for the song reached a new level when I saw how it moved people at the Black Family Reunion Celebration, which the National Council of Negro Women inaugurated in 1986. We created this event as a weekend during which people from all walks of life could come together for educational and cultural activities to counter the stereotypes and pervasive negative images of the "vanishing" black family in the media and in our society.

Melba Moore, the renowned soprano, traveled with the celebration across the country for several years. She sang the song at every major event throughout the weekends. It never failed. Large groups, small groups, and even crowds of tens of thousands of people stood together, transformed in the spirit of our shared historic strengths and value traditions of the black family. "Lift Every Voice and Sing," in tandem with "The Black Family Reunion Pledge" (written by Maya Angelou), became a call to action inspiring all to

*Saturday afternoon in the pool hall, Clarksdale, Mississippi, c. 1940s.* Courtesy of Schomburg Center for Research in Black Culture, The New York Public Library

recognize and utilize tools for betterment. Many have testified that their experience at the Black Family Reunion has been a catalyst for profound personal change. To date, more than fifteen million people in eight regional celebrations have participated without a single police incident. To provide everyone with opportunities such as these becomes even more important in this millennium.

We have come a long way since I first recited "Lift Every Voice and Sing," yet we still have a long way to go. The climate of righteous indignation about injustice has changed since the March on Washington in 1963. Instead, the African American experience today continues to be marked with great expectations and frustrations.

The progress cannot be denied nor dare we overlook the plight of the masses of people. Our young people can benefit from using the song as a text to understand the stormy past and even the truth about slavery. Every time I sing "Lift Every Voice," I find it can help bring new strength to move in the spirit of the song with the commitment to march on till victory is won!

# ALEXIS M. HERMAN

U.S. secretary of labor

As a young girl growing up in Alabama, I first saw the state capitol from a housing project in Montgomery where my mother lived with my great-aunt while attending Alabama State University. Back then, the only view I had of my state's capitol was from the outside.

My mother followed her dream and became a teacher. And seeing her fulfill her goal helped me to see the capitol as a place of possibility. Today, I envision her looking down and saying, "Alexis, you were right."

My father was a trailblazer. He was the first African American elected official in post-Reconstruction Alabama. He was a Democratic wardsman—the only office open to an African American at that time. Through his eyes, I saw my capitol as a place of power,

*Street scene, Holmes County, Mississippi, c. 1940s.* Courtesy of Schomburg Center for Research in Black Culture, The New York Public Library

and of potential. If he were here, he would echo my mother, and say, "Alexis, you were right."

For me, "Lift Every Voice and Sing" symbolizes the possibilities, power, and potential I witnessed through the accomplishments of my parents. But most of all, it is about how a resilient spirit, a sense of purpose, and faith in God can overcome nearly any obstacle.

Today, we are basking in the rising sun of a new millennium. America has overcome many of the obvious obstacles that inspired James Weldon Johnson, and there is much to celebrate. Unemployment is at a record low. The economy is the strongest it's been in a generation.

But we know the light of prosperity isn't shining in every community. Too many people are being left behind, in neighborhoods that are being left out. That is why the Negro National Anthem is more than an anthem of hope and progress for African Americans. It is a reminder of our shared responsibility for keeping our nation moving in the right direction—whether our ancestors first glimpsed this country from an auction block or from Ellis Island.

By reminding us of our responsibility to one another, and of the strength, sacrifices, and accomplishments of those on whose shoulders we stand, James Weldon Johnson also reminds us that we must equip every young person with the skills, values, energy, and commitment to lift his or her voice in government, in business, in the classroom, in places of worship, and around the dinner table, so our nation's prosperity will soar to every citizen and every community.

*W. E. B. Du Bois, Fisk University, Nashville, Tennessee, c. 1940s.* Courtesy of Schomburg Center for Research in Black Culture,
The New York Public Library

# FRANCES HOOKS

retired educator

# BENJAMIN L. HOOKS

former executive director, NAACP

We have often read the story of how James Weldon Johnson and J. Rosamond Johnson wrote "Lift Every Voice and Sing." Having discussed the origin of the song on numerous occasions between ourselves and with others, we understood that this was poetry and music of the highest order. The fact that the song was written by two young black men—twenty-eight-year-old James Weldon Johnson and twenty-six-year-old J. Rosamond Johnson—will give any person pause. The kind of inspiration that flowed through the creative veins of the Johnson brothers happens only rarely.

Listen to the words: they could very well be the American national anthem, dealing with the historical movement of this nation. The song speaks about liberty and rejoicing. It evokes the history of change in a nation filled with immigrant Americans, who came here with and without their consent: their dark paths trod, their triumphs achieved, and many of their hopes and dreams still to be realized.

We African Americans are too often despondent about the slow progress of race relations; however, we must remain sustained and comforted by the faith that James Weldon Johnson displayed one hundred years ago. If he believed in the promise of this land when he wrote "Lift Every Voice and Sing," only thirty-five years after slavery ended, then surely today we must keep that hope alive.

We have sung the Negro National Anthem countless times, yet each time it never ceases to renew our spirits and strengthen our resolve to fight on.

Thank you, Johnson brothers, for an enduring treasure.

# LENA HORNE

entertainer

I was a young woman during the 1930s, and the crude realities of Jim Crow in Hollywood were overtly wretched for me and other African American actors. In those years the unsubtle Jim Crow system, which Hollywood perpetuated, entrenched stereotypes of blacks in American films.

Being reared in a family filled with activists gave me the incentive and courage to stay in Hollywood *and* reject its Jim Crow system. My activist grandmother Cora Calhoun Horne, an early member of the NAACP and the woman suffrage movement, and my uncle the reformer-poet Frank Horne both knew James Weldon Johnson. Grandmother added my name to the NAACP membership rolls when I was only two years of age. Thereupon I attended many NAACP events, where "Lift Every Voice and Sing" was always sung. The song was a symbol of racial solidarity in the Horne family for as long as I can remember.

Writing about the song that we African Americans call the Negro National Anthem evokes so many memories—the March on Washington and marching with Medgar Evers. I shall not forget the valor of Medgar Evers. Marching with him during the turbulent 1960s for fair employment opportunities, desegregation of public accommodations, and the right to vote enabled me to better understand the black struggle. We marched knowing that, for any of us, death could become a reality within seconds. In this nation, murder was too often the answer to those blacks who "stepped out of their place" simply by seeking their constitutional rights. Yet, for a hundred years, "Lift Every Voice and Sing" has been the cuirass that protected the hopes and aspirations of a people in the face of the forces of evil.

For me, "Lift Every Voice and Sing" signifies that our dream of racial harmony will one day come to pass and America will truly be the land of the *free*.

*Peanut vendor, Harlem, 1949.* Courtesy of Schomburg Center for Research in Black Culture, The New York Public Library

# MILDRED J. HUDSON

*education reform expert, author*

My oldest sister, Mildverta (pronounced *Mill-verta*) Hudson Shead, remembers singing "Lift Every Voice and Sing" as early as 1941. That was two years before I was born, so I imagine I heard the song before my birth. We sang it in our small wooden church and at the beginning of each school day. Surrounded by thick willows, pecan trees, oaks, and pines, we crawled under our one-room schoolhouse and sang the song during school recess. At home, my mother, Willie Ester Wright Hudson, born in 1912, would sing "Lift Every Voice" as she went about her daily chores. She would lift her proud brown chin and strike the perfect note as she reinforced what had by then become our family's dream: "Let us march on till victory is won." We desperately needed that song.

I grew up in a segregated black world of rich soil, pungent gospel flavor, and swinging in the rhythm of the blues. But it was also a world where the KKK ruled and black men often found themselves facing death with a noose around their neck. Back then in Tunica County, Mississippi—now famous for its rich gambling casinos—we embraced the Johnson brothers' song as valuable information from the outside world. It also soothed our hearts, pointed the way for how we have tried to live our lives, raise our children, and help pave the road for others.

We were independent farmers back then and found solace in "Lift Every Voice and Sing" when our relatives were arrested for having too much knowledge, making money, owning land, driving new cars, or wanting to vote. There were times, however, when America was so cruel that almost nothing could prevent our despair and feeling of helplessness. The entire world cannot forget what happened to my distant cousin, Emmett Till, now frozen in history at age fourteen, and how he was brutally murdered in 1955 for allegedly whistling at a white woman. I was twelve years old when Emmett was slaughtered, and I remember thinking that God *and* nature had conspired against us. As a child, of course, I did not

*Walter Francis White, executive secretary of the NAACP, early 1950s.* Collection of
Jane White Viazzi

have many ways to analyze national issues or ask the right questions, but singing the right songs helped.

In July 1999, over 150 of our relatives came together in Chicago to celebrate our survival at a family reunion. Now my siblings and I are members of the oldest living generation, and two-thirds of the family seems to be under the age of ten. Screaming, running, dancing, jumping, and playing, the Hudson children had a zest for life that appeared uncontrollable at times, and by late afternoon of the second day of the reunion, it crossed my mind that perhaps some of the children had adopted inappropriate values.

"Shhh, shhh," I heard my sister Mildverta say quietly as she stood tall and imposing and dignified at the front of the large room. "Let us sing." I stood along with the rest of the family and watched my sister slowly transform the noise in the room into a 150-person symphony:

> *Sing a song full of the faith that the dark past has taught us,*
> *Sing a song full of the hope that the present has brought us,*
> *Facing the rising sun of our new day begun*
> *Let us march on till victory is won.*

I work hard at marching on because I know what America once was and what it sometimes yearns to be. That is why I have been able to help develop close to $200 million in education programs for low-income communities, and why I write, consult, and serve as an advocate for poor children everywhere. It is no accident that President Bill Clinton adopted my teacher recruitment and preparation program as a model for the nation's public schools. I know how important our songs, traditions, and education are to our survival.

At the reunion, more than one hundred little Hudson family children stood quietly with great dignity, then raised their proud chins, as my mother had in the 1940s, to sing *our* national anthem. We have passed along one of our most powerful secret weapons to yet another generation. We are now four generations and counting.

*"Repent, and be baptized every one of you": Baptism, c. 1950s.* Photograph by John W. Mosley, courtesy of the Charles L. Blockson Afro-American Collection, Temple University

# JESSE JACKSON

civil rights activist and minister

In 1984, I founded the Rainbow Coalition, grounding it in cultural diversity as the basis of my presidential campaign. The coalition reflected not only the way I see America but, more important, the way that I think that the struggle for justice has to unfold among those who have suffered from many forms of disadvantage. This concept, therefore, reflects my continuing commitment to the progressive agenda of the Rainbow/PUSH Coalition. Traditionally, to begin our Saturday morning forum, we honor our culture through the Negro National Anthem, "Lift Every Voice and Sing," because it exemplifies the human spirit and the pride of millions of African Americans. It is immersed in the deep imageries of a history past, and yet it provides hope, continued courage, and determination to stand as one.

I learned in the civil rights movement that the most powerful manifestation of the struggle for justice came when people of all colors came together to pool their power, with the same purpose of ridding the country of the scourge of racism and forging a new concept of freedom for everyone. I say "everyone" meaning also those who manage the system of oppression, a position taken in the civil rights movement by Dr. Martin Luther King, Jr., and reinforced by Nelson Mandela when he emerged into the sunlight of freedom, after having been jailed for twenty-seven years, holding the hand of his white jailer. This view reflected the understanding of our movement, that in order to hold a man down in a ditch, you must get into the ditch with him. So, if the oppressed is able to free herself, she also frees her oppressor from the indignity of that situation.

Some of the most dramatic events that the popular history of the civil rights movement has not captured were individual acts of courage by persons who simply made up their mind to act because freedom was a precious thing that would not be obtained as a gift from someone else. The enactment of song represents a presence of solidarity, even a sword of benevolence. Having freedom, one comes to understand how deeply its attainment depended upon one's own personal commitment to do something that would bring about change.

The results of this movement were concrete. The 1964 Civil Rights Act, the 1965 Voting Rights Act, the 1968 Civil Rights Act mandating fair housing, and affirmative action. Through these laws, many people of all colors have been able to achieve upward mobility in society. Blacks have benefited from laws which made it unlawful to discriminate in hiring and promotion, in buying a house, in voting and holding office, and in seeking higher education. As a result, the black middle class has grown, achieving ever greater breakthroughs in every field of employment; the number of black elected officials has grown from 250, at the time the Voting Rights Act was passed, to nearly 9,000 today; currently, there are 38 black members of Congress. Also, there are 1.1 million blacks in America's colleges and universities.

The dignity of race and the richness of its legacy to America is a fundamental key to our social progress since the encounter of the European and the Native American. We must recognize that this fact is the way to the future and that racism is the path to the past.

## VERNON JARRETT

journalist

It took one epiphany after another for me, a fledgling journalist, to thoroughly appreciate America's greatest soul hymn: "Lift Every Voice and Sing."

It required many a recollection of those wonderful older folk of my childhood in Tennessee and later conversations with several of our elder black scholars to appreciate the insights that James Weldon Johnson capsulized in his powerful poem/song.

The old folks? Yes. How they stood promptly and proudly when they sang "our anthem": profound expressions on withered faces with misty eyes that reflected years of travail, survival, and small

*Jacob M. Nhlapo, South African educator, speaking to students at Livingstone College in Salisbury, North Carolina, 1950s.* Courtesy of Schomburg Center for Research in Black Culture, The New York Public Library

triumphs. Eyes that glanced down at us little people standing at their sides, trying to sing along with them—even though we, like them, didn't know all the words.

However, there were times when Johnson's lyrics provoked annoying questions, particularly after I grew up, went off to college, and became absorbed in history and the editing of our campus newspaper, the *Knoxville College Aurora.*

Big contradictions appeared when I learned that Johnson had written "Lift Every Voice" while living in Florida during that mean centennial year 1900. It was that wide chasm which separated Johnson's "new day begun" from the racial realities of his day.

What new day? The first year of the twentieth century was being blighted by more unwashed bloody white hands, red and sooty from 105 lynchings—*20 more than in the previous year.*

In 1900, racism had become so ignored or acceptable in white America that Senator "Pitchfork" Ben Tillman of South Carolina felt comfortable and void of contrition when he stood on the Senate floor and bragged about how his state kept blacks from voting. His words:

*"We have done our best. We have scratched our heads to find out how we could eliminate the last one of them. We have stuffed ballot boxes. We shot them. We are not ashamed."*

Learning of that speech provoked a recollection of poet Countee Cullen's question of how God could "make a poet black and bid him sing." Yet Johnson's song spoke of a "rising sun" and "the hope that the present has brought us." The truth was that our sun had been eclipsed four years earlier by a Supreme Court ruling of May 18, 1896, *Plessy v. Ferguson.*

New day? In 1900, the Confederate states were en route to, if not finished with, undoing all "Black Reconstruction" state constitutions by saturating them with Jim Crow statutes.

I began to fathom Johnson's insights in the summer of 1975, during an interview of the late Dr. Benjamin E. Mays, president emeritus of Morehouse College. He had just turned eighty-one. I asked him to consider the most profound achievement of blacks in America.

*Singer Eartha Kitt, 1950s.* Photograph by John W. Mosley, courtesy of The Charles L. Blockson Afro-American Collection, Temple University

His answer was reflective:

*"Our greatest achievement has been our refusal to commit suicide—biologically, spiritually, or intellectually. Regardless of how disguised the invitations, the great majority of us always have rejected the temptation to give up hope and to self-destruct."*

Dr. Mays's statement summoned Dr. W. E. B. Du Bois's 1960 warning to social science teachers about disguised temptations to accept black oblivion. Du Bois had advised:

*"I am not fighting to settle the question of racial equality in America by the process of getting rid of the Negro race, getting rid of black folk, not producing black children, forgetting the slave trade and slavery and the struggle for emancipation, or forgetting abolition and especially of ignoring the whole cultural history of Africans in the World."*

In Johnson's lyrics one could remember, witness, and become inspired by "our whole cultural history."

Today "Lift Every Voice" is our quintessential pledge of allegiance to the Flag of Universal Humanity.

It is our bold Black Manifesto for a New Millennium.

# MAE JEMISON

former astronaut

To open one's mouth and sing with emotion and enthusiasm is among the most liberating and fulfilling acts that we humans can do. The words and notes we sing translate our mood and thoughts into vibrations that fill the space around us with images, possibilities, and ideals.

In the fourth grade, 1965, when I learned "Lift Every Voice and Sing"—the Negro National Anthem—I thought, "This is going to be a difficult song to learn." I did not know the definition of all the words. I could not carry the tune of even the simplest songs. But over the years, I learned the words and the tune. Still, I always got confused by the phrases "Full of the faith that the dark past has

*Dr. Horace Mann Bond, president of Lincoln University, presents an honorary degree to Albert Einstein, 1950s.* Photograph
by John W. Mosley, courtesy of The Charles L. Blockson Afro-American Collection, Temple University

taught us" and "Full of the hope that the present has brought us." The words "faith" and "hope." Their meaning.

Faith is that knowledge we carry deep inside ourselves that guides us along a path to a brighter day. We know which turns to take on the path, no matter how cold, dark, steep, or treacherous.

And once we reach a clearer day with light around us, hope refreshes and energizes us. Hope gives us that new wind, extra breath to continue our vision.

Now I know that "victory is won" when each day I can look around me and remember to sing of the possibilities.

## CHARLES JOHNSON

scholar and novelist

In the 1950s, in a little African Methodist Episcopal church in Evanston, Illinois, I first heard our choir perform "Lift Every Voice and Sing." If memory serves, I was an eight-year-old seated on a hard wooden bench between my parents, both wearing their go-to-meeting best, and I asked my mother what this particular song was about. "Just listen," she said, gently elbowing me into silence as the choir sang James Weldon Johnson's words, her voice filling suddenly with the sort of respect she reserved for things hymnal and holy. "*This,*" she informed me, "is the Negro National Anthem."

This, her tone said, is important.

Mom's explanation that Sunday morning, and her reaction, initially brought me more confusion than clarity. Didn't we, as Americans, already have a national anthem? And why, I wondered, did my mother, a bibliophile with the soul of an actress, a woman who was wonderfully ironic, occasionally cynical, and capable of devastating scorn for whatever she saw as hypocritical and phony, all but stand up and salute when this lay's last lines alchemized the air? Its simplicity was deceptive. In a way I could not unlock forty years ago, my mother was saying that it was necessary for me to understand this poem if I wanted to grasp something essential about her, my father—and myself.

Looking back, during Black History Month, I believe now that her affection for this ineluctable work, which celebrated its *hundredth birthday on February 12, 2000,* consisted partly of a profound appreciation for its perennial, much-honored place in black culture, and partly of her deeply felt gratitude for the towering figure, the (Harlem) Renaissance man, who produced it as, in his own words, "an incidental effort, an effort made under stress and with no intention other than to meet the needs of a particular moment."

James Weldon Johnson is best known for his poetry, his stewardship of the National Association for the Advancement of Colored People, and his classic novel about the perils of passing for white, *The Autobiography of an Ex-Colored Man* (first published anonymously in 1912, then reissued with his authorship acknowledged in 1927). But the spirit of his remarkable life, influential aesthetics, and formidable political legacy is as fully contained in "Lift Every Voice and Sing" as in his major literary and social contributions.

In "Lift Every Voice and Sing," elder Johnson gave Americans, black and white, that rarest of literary gifts—a song worthy of singing for a century.

## GUY JOHNSON

novelist

I've never been a singer. "Can't carry a melody in a bucket" doesn't begin to reflect my inability to stay in key. Thus, I've never made an effort to learn all the words of songs. A few lyrics may stay in my mind, but that's not the consequence of conscious effort. Despite this disability, music has been an important part of my life. In the early seventies, I even played rhythm guitar for a couple of years in a Top 40 band. Experts are still trying to understand how I accomplished this feat. I imagine when they succeed in finding out how

*Horseback riding, c. 1950s.* Photograph by John W. Mosley, courtesy of The Charles L. Blockson Afro-American Collection, Temple University

Strom Thurmond got an award for civil rights, they may find the answer. Yet one song stands out above all others: "Lift Every Voice and Sing."

In my earliest glimmerings, before I knew what it meant to be black in America, and long before I was awakened to the duties and responsibilities of being a man, I knew the importance of the Negro National Anthem. I learned this song's significance from my family. They were an eclectic mix of blue-collar workers, Bible thumpers, cut-and-shoots, and freethinkers. There were only three things for which all members of that disparate group would stand up without question. The first was God, the second was the American flag, and the third was "Lift Every Voice and Sing." Although these were straight-backed people who fiercely prized their individual dignity, they always seemed to stand straighter when they sang this song.

I remember one particular occasion in the early sixties when my mother (Dr. Maya Angelou) headed the New York office of the SCLC for Dr. Martin Luther King. Dr. King had come to town for an important fund-raising effort and as a student activist I had been invited to the initial strategy meeting. The meeting was convened with a prayer and "Lift Every Voice." By the time we got to the second verse I had wandered so far off key, I may have been singing the first strains of the "She's Too Fat for Me Polka." Eventually I sputtered into silence. My mother edged over to me and whispered, "Keep on singing! As long as you take the poetry and the spirit of the song to heart, the authors couldn't ask for more."

Today I still can't sing, but I know all the words to this song. They are part of my bones and marrow and they flow through my thoughts like life-giving blood.

*Educator and civic leader Mary McLeod Bethune greets ballplayer Jackie Robinson, 1950s.* Photograph by John W. Mosley, courtesy of The Charles L. Blockson Afro-American Collection, Temple University

# JOHN JOHNSON

publisher, *Ebony* magazine

As I explained in my book, *Succeeding Against the Odds*, there were few models of hope in Arkansas City, Arkansas, where I spent the first years of my life. One of these models was a song that was different from anything I had ever heard before.

I don't remember where or when I heard the song for the first time. I think it was in the Arkansas City Colored School or the St. John Baptist Church. But wherever I heard it, I was lifted up and transformed by the majestic, empowering harmonies of "Lift Every Voice and Sing," calling us to "march on till victory is won."

And I remember being secretly thrilled by the fact that the song was written by two great men named Johnson—James Weldon Johnson and his brother, J. Rosamond Johnson. The song followed me to Chicago and was one of the inspirations for the founding of my first magazine, *Negro Digest*.

Over the years, the song and the message have become a part of the message and the mission of the Johnson Publishing Company and especially our two major magazines, *Ebony* and *Jet*. Strangely and significantly, "Lift Every Voice and Sing" is more relevant in 2000 than it was in 1900, for there has never been a greater need for blacks and their allies to "face the rising sun of our new day begun."

# KEVIN JOHNSON

professional basketball player

It stirred my heart. It uplifted my spirit. I remember I stood silently in the church sanctuary, transfixed by the soaring voices of the choir as they sang the powerful lyrics and music of "Lift Every Voice and Sing."

"Lift Every Voice and Sing" pays homage to the brave African

*Into the pool, c. 1950s.* Photograph by John W. Mosley, courtesy of The Charles L. Blockson Afro-American Collection, Temple University

*Coeds in Atlantic City, c. 1960s.* Photograph by John W. Mosley, courtesy of The Charles L. Blockson Afro-American Collection, Temple University

American men and women who never gave up their faith or the prospect of a better tomorrow, despite unspeakable pain and suffering. The freedom and success many of us enjoy today would not be possible if our ancestors had given up hope.

The lyrics are humbling insofar as they recall the selfless sacrifices of Harriet Tubman, Sojourner Truth, Frederick Douglass, Dr. Martin Luther King, Jr., and countless unknown soldiers in the fight for racial freedom and equality. It is upon their broad shoulders that we stand.

Upon reflecting on their legacy, I was inspired to found St. HOPE Academy, a youth development center. When I considered how the people who relentlessly fought for racial freedom paved the way for me, I knew I had a responsibility—that of positively shaping the lives of children—much more important than playing in the NBA. I was confident that I could offer children the opportunity to enrich their present lives by unlocking their past.

My hope was to give the children that which was given to me when I went away to the University of California–Berkeley: the desire to learn. It was in this enriching college environment that my interests in history and lifelong learning were first sparked. I experienced firsthand the liberation of delving into one's own history. There was no doubt in my mind that St. HOPE Academy must help young people discover their own history so they might realize the spirit of human striving and, in turn, understand their own limitless potential.

As the children of St. HOPE Academy lift their voices and sing of the proud legacy of their ancestors, they celebrate a spirit that cannot be destroyed and a hope that cannot be plucked from their hearts no matter what their circumstances. Within this song lies the spirit of life, the spirit of boldness, the spirit of God.

We aim to make St. HOPE Academy an institution that serves as a beacon of hope for future generations. Moreover, we aim to make St. HOPE Academy a timeless institution in which the principles and ideas embodied in "Lift Every Voice and Sing" are instilled in our children. For we believe that, more than anything

*Wilt Chamberlain (center), guarded by Bill Russell (left), 1960s.* Photograph by John W. Mosley, courtesy of The Charles L. Blockson Afro-American Collection, Temple University

else, "Lift Every Voice and Sing" provides words of hope. It does more than simply leave a vague melody in our hearts. It propels us forward. It grants each new generation the hope of human strength, dignity, and progress.

# NATHANIEL R. JONES

federal judge

I offer this testimonial in recognition of the debt black Americans owe for the inspiration bequeathed by the James Weldon Johnson–J. Rosamond Johnson collaborative composition "Lift Every Voice and Sing," which is both a call to battle and a fervent prayer. One of my earliest memories is of sitting in the front row at NAACP civil rights forums in my hometown of Youngstown, Ohio, taking in the flow of challenging speeches at programs bracketed by the stirring song, so universally sung that it is regarded as the Negro National Anthem. At an early age, I was inspired by that song to join, through the NAACP Youth Council, the battle against segregation. During that period of my life, the Supreme Court decision in *Plessy v. Ferguson* was giving constitutional legitimacy to racial segregation. In that bleak period, the lyrics of the Johnson brothers exhorted us to lift our voices and keep the faith that we had learned in the past.

Those exhorting words of the brilliant Johnson brothers gave us strength and resolve. The likes of Walter White, Roy Wilkins, William H. Hastie, and Charles Hamilton Houston and his protégé Thurgood Marshall were among those inspired to fashion battle strategies that would challenge the segregation system propped up by the mythology of white supremacy and black inferiority. The song was sung in churches and at civil rights meetings large and small, in lodge halls, at colleges, at union meetings, and wherever people gathered, determined to "march on till victory [was] won."

The most important legal victory of the twentieth century, *Brown v. Board of Education,* was won by the NAACP in 1954. This

*The Supremes in performance: Florence Ballard, Mary Wilson, and Diana Ross, 1960s.* Courtesy of Schomburg Center for Research in Black Culture, The New York Public Library

culmination of the long battle fought over "stony roads" represented a watershed. Slowly, black Americans saw and felt changes in a wide number of fields—education, housing, and voting rights; in the workplace; during interstate and intrastate travel; and in places of public accommodation. Yet, even while celebrating, black Americans still recognized that much work remained to be done.

In the triumphant post-*Brown* period, when I, as successor to Houston, Marshall, and Robert L. Carter, was privileged to serve as chief legal counsel of the National Association for the Advancement of Colored People, the tie that bound people across generational, geographical, and social lines in the struggle to remove vestiges of *Plessy v. Ferguson,* from my youth to my days as chief counsel, was "Lift Every Voice and Sing."

Sadly, the gains realized have been placed at risk. Recent court rulings, which strikingly replicate those that gave rise to Jim Crow in its most wretched and subtle forms, threaten a return to racial segregation. Many beneficiaries of the long struggle, who, for whatever reason, are now accommodating to resegregation, need to be reminded of the prayer in the final stanza of "Lift Every Voice and Sing":

> *God of our weary years,*
> *God of our silent tears,*
> *Thou who has brought us thus far on the way;*
> *Keep us forever in the path, we pray.*
> *Lest our feet stray from the places, our God, where we met*
> *    Thee,*
> *Lest our hearts, drunk with the wine of the world, we forget*
> *    Thee,*
> *Shadowed beneath Thy hand,*
> *May we forever stand,*
> *True to our God*
> *True to our native land.*

Amen.

# QUINCY JONES

composer and producer

Over the course of my life, I've realized that if there are any common denominators in the world, they are spirituality and musicality. I've always gone for music that gives me goose bumps—music that touches my heart and my soul. "Lift Every Voice and Sing" brings to the fore of my being such innate and visible sensations.

I was born in Chicago in the 1930s. My father moved our family to Bremerton, Washington (a suburb of Seattle), during the early 1940s. It was during these years that I developed a strong interest in music. Later, while in junior high school, I began to play the trumpet and sang in a Gospel quartet. It was most likely during this time when I first heard "Lift Every Voice and Sing" in church. At such a tender age, the song's words and music didn't move me as they would in later years.

As I grew into manhood and began to realize the social and political strife that had permeated our nation and the world for centuries, songs like "Lift Every Voice and Sing" became important in my life and in the lives of other African Americans around me. By this time, I had developed a keen awareness of the elements that give a song depth, meaning, and longevity. It's not "rocket science." For me sincerity is essential in songs. If the lyrics truly reveal the writer's heart and soul, the song will communicate that spirituality. "Lift Every Voice and Sing" holds this unique capacity. James Weldon Johnson and J. Rosamond Johnson gave us this noble song to soothe our emotional wounds while, simultaneously, lifting our spirits.

When I look back, there is that spiritually uplifting song that became increasingly important in my life. Today, I look forward with hope that those of us who are familiar with the Negro National Anthem and those who come to know it will find comfort in the power of its music and the motivation in its lyrics. I am optimistic about such a desire because I strongly believe in James Weldon Johnson's vision of a color-blind America.

*Young men and women of the Jack and Jill Association pose after a dance, c. 1960s.* Photograph by John W. Mosley, courtesy of

The Charles L. Blockson Afro-American Collection, Temple University

# DAMON J. KEITH

federal judge

While America proclaims color blindness and individuality for all, racism continues to disfigure our day-to-day existence. The following merely suggest our historical reality:

- James Byrd, an African American man, was beaten, hooked to a truck, and dragged to his death.
- A white supremacist went on a shooting spree in Illinois and Indiana, killing two persons and injuring twelve others, all of whom were either persons of color or Jewish.
- Amadou Diallo, a black man, unarmed and outside his home, was shot nineteen times and killed by police.
- A white police officer pled guilty to sodomizing Abner Louima, a black man, with a broomstick while another officer held him down in a Brooklyn station house bathroom.
- African Americans are almost twice as likely as Caucasians to suffer a stroke, according to a joint Harvard and Duke University study.
- Denny's Restaurant reached a settlement for $46 million after failing to serve African American Secret Service agents.

The pain and pervasiveness of incidents like these led Arthur Ashe to explain that the difficulty of being black in America outweighed the burden of living with AIDS or HIV.

Despite the brutal reality we have endured, despair has never defeated us. When James Weldon Johnson and J. Rosamond Johnson created "Lift Every Voice and Sing," African Americans were enduring an even more dismal reality. Our survival and perseverance under these conditions reflect our unparalleled strength of will and ability to overcome despair.

Optimism has sustained African Americans throughout our dark and desolate history. If we lose that, all is lost. "Lift Every Voice and Sing" articulates our triumph over oppression, adversity,

*Martin Luther King, Jr., embracing his wife, Coretta Scott King, 1960s.* Courtesy of Schomburg Center for Research in Black Culture, The New York Public Library

and cruel neglect. The song constantly reminds us as a people that we have eternal optimism when there is little to be optimistic about. The song reassures us that although tears have watered the "weary years," we must "march on till victory is won."

As we embrace a new millennium, we have so much for which to be grateful. We must continue exercising our God-given power with grace, humility, and understanding. We must never deny that "all Men [and Women] are created equal, that they are endowed by their Creator with certain unalienable Rights, that among these are Life, Liberty, and the Pursuit of Happiness." For our work is not done until we have lifted every voice and enabled it to sing.

We ask today, as Johnson inspired us to do: Lord, "keep us forever in the path."

# MARTIN L. KILSON, JR.

political-science professor, Harvard University

Born in 1931, I grew up in a small mill town named Ambler, in Montgomery County, Pennsylvania—the same county that Charles Blockson grew up in. Within thirty miles of Philadelphia, Ambler had in 1910 2,649 persons, of whom 10 percent (266) were African Americans, 40 percent Italian Americans, and 40 percent White Anglo-Saxon Protestants (WASPs). A wealthy WASP family—the Mattisons—owned a textile mill (Keasbey & Mattison) and also built in the 1880s one of those Gilded Age castlelike mansions, on a 250-acre estate at the north end of town.

The African American community that I grew up in was founded by former Civil War veterans (one was my great-grandfather Jacob Laws) who settled initially in a village adjacent to Ambler named Penllyn, a former Underground Railroad stop. A few black families moved just several miles in the 1880s to neighboring Ambler, where they worked as chauffeurs, artisans, valets, caterers, and maids for the Mattisons and other elite WASP families (the Knights, Houghs, Biddles, and so on). In 1885 blacks built an

*Thurgood Marshall greets an unidentified African leader and his wife, c. 1960s.* Courtesy of the Schomburg Center for Research in Black Culture, The New York Public Library

African Union Methodist Protestant church, and in this AUMP church I first discovered the soulful and haunting anthem of black freedom and black honor authored by James Weldon and J. Rosamond Johnson—"Lift Every Voice and Sing."

The Ambler/Penllyn black population was a joint community for many purposes, so while Penllyn children had to go to a segregated elementary school, they went on to integrated middle and high schools in Ambler. There were two black schoolteachers, Mrs. Helen Perry Moore and Mrs. Evelyn Brown Wright. Mrs. Moore, who ran the Penllyn elementary school, preached a get-up-and-go ethos to black children, and used our great black freedom anthem, "Lift Every Voice," to communicate this ethos at the school-year opening ceremony, on Armistice Day, on Lincoln's Birthday, and during Negro History Week.

That get-up-and-go ethos also pervaded the Ambler black community, and our black freedom anthem was used to communicate it. "Lift Every Voice and Sing" gave us motivational strength and a sense of our black ethnic worth. This occurred, however, not in Ambler's public schools but in the AUMP church, which in the 1930s was pastored by my father, the Reverend Martin Luther Kilson, Sr. The AUMP church also housed the Boy Scout troop for the Ambler/Penllyn black community, and our scoutmaster—Mr. Millard Scott—had us sing "Lift Every Voice and Sing" at the close of Scout meetings, while at the start we sang "The Star-Spangled Banner." Also, "Lift Every Voice and Sing" was sung at meetings of the Women's Auxiliary group at the AUMP church, which was run by a church stalwart, Mrs. Annie Lane.

Finally, testimony to the enormous stimulation that we black children derived from singing "Lift Every Voice And Sing" can be found in the sizable number of Ambler/Penllyn black children who climbed the social mobility ladder to the middle class and professional class. I have in mind the following:

· Helen Perry Moore and Evelyn Brown Wright were school teachers by the 1930s.

- Rex Gorleigh was a nationally recognized black artist by the 1940s.
- Ruby Rose became a lieutenant colonel in the U.S. Women's Army Nurse Corps.
- Anita Moore Hackney became a college administrator in the 1960s.
- Clement Cottingham and I became political scientists in the 1960s.
- Constance Cottingham became a mathematician in the 1960s.
- Walter Moore became a schoolteacher in the 1960s.
- Kevin Flowers became a lawyer in the 1960s.

This list represents just a few of the achievers out of the black community of my boyhood years. All of us from Ambler/Penllyn know one thing for certain: We owe a special debt for motivation, self-esteem, and courage to the Johnson brothers' anthem of black freedom and honor.

# KNIGHT A. KIPLINGER

president, Kiplinger Washington Editors, Inc.

When I first read the lyrics of "Lift Every Voice and Sing," back in the turbulent sixties, I was stunned to see that the song had been written in 1900. Why? Because the words were so joyous and hopeful, but 1900 was definitely *not* a time of celebration for American Negroes as a group. A series of Supreme Court cases in the 1880s and 1890s had disenfranchised Southern blacks and allowed segregation in public and private facilities. Lynchings of Negroes were occurring at a rate of more than 150 a year.

But here comes James Weldon Johnson, twenty-nine years old, urging his people to rejoice and "sing a song full of the hope that the present has brought us." Was Johnson a fool? Was he oblivious

*Mr. and Mrs. William Pinckney enjoy a wedding toast, 1960s.* Courtesy of Schomburg Center for Research in Black Culture, The New York Public Library

to the worsening political plight of his fellow African Americans? Not at all. He was simply exhibiting a classic American trait—unquenchable optimism. To him, the glass of human progress was always half full, not half empty. He saw and was heartened by the amazing economic strides that his race had made in the thirty-five years since the end of slavery, especially the emergence of a black middle class of college-educated professionals and business owners—a class to which he belonged.

The optimism he showed in "Lift Every Voice and Sing" fore-shadowed the positive events that would unfold in the next decade: the Niagara Movement, the founding of the NAACP, and the coming together of a new American coalition—whites and blacks, Christians and Jews—committed to justice for all races. When Johnson urged his fellow Negroes to "forever stand . . . True to our native land," he didn't mean Africa, as Marcus Garvey would mean twenty years later. Johnson's only native land was his beloved America. He believed that this nation, for all its imperfections, offered the world's best hope for the eventual creation of a just, multiracial society. In this belief he was prophetic.

One hundred years after the writing of "Lift Every Voice and Sing," American people of color—individually and collectively—have achieved successes Johnson could only have dreamed of. When Americans get discouraged over racial tensions today and in the future, we should remember the faith that Johnson showed amid circumstances far bleaker. He urged us to "march on till victory is won." We Americans will be marching forever, of course, because there is never a final victory. New obstacles appear, the battleground shifts, new goals are set. Like the poet Johnson, we should simply recognize and savor the hundreds of small victories that, taken together, constitute human progress.

# YAPHET KOTTO

*actor*

It may not be popular in this day of idealism and attempted social reforms to suggest that individuals do their share in helping to make humanity's great dreams come true, but certainly there can be no harm in such an appeal. After all is said and done (mostly said), no governmental, social, or religious system, arbitrarily established, can save humanity unless, first, the system be wholesome, and, second, the individuals who function under the system help to make it work.

Reformers, including well-meaning politicians, preachers, and teachers, have their own good place in the world, but history attests to the fact that no reformer can make folks be good, and that the best and the greatest thing any teacher ever accomplished was to persuade individuals to take a good look at themselves and be willing to assume responsibility for their conduct and its consequences. There is a destiny that shapes our ends, but that destiny is determined by ourselves, not by any leader, ruler, angel, demon, government, or god. It is time that we stop placing the blame for our troubles upon someone or something outside ourselves. It is time to say we are Americans. Not just African Americans. It is time to sing the National Anthem as well as "Lift Every Voice and Sing."

There is a God, and that deity has given to man everything that he needs, including mind, and the power of will to make his life a thing of beauty and joy. However, the very possession of willpower absolves God from any part in the sorrows and tragedies that come to man through his failure to exercise that godlike attribute of his being. He who employs that power for his own and his fellow man's uplift and for the glory of his Creator finally becomes a conqueror, and even in the stress of modern life, with its apparent injustices and inequalities, he stands serene, untouched.

It is not the ebony-skinned Uncle Tom but his "master" Simon Legree who is the slave. If you are St. Paul, you will sing in prison. If you are a tyrant, you will tremble with fear, even though you be

*Members of Morgan State College's track team pose during the Penn Relays, c. 1960s.* Photograph by John W. Mosley, courtesy of The Charles L. Blockson Afro-American Collection, Temple University

surrounded by purchased servants and a million "luxuries." What I make of my life is up to me. What you make of your life is up to you. The great teachers, saints, and sages are to be revered, but none of them can save us unless we abide by the good laws they give us. "I leave you now," said Buddha. "Be lamps unto yourselves."

# GWENDOLYN KNIGHT LAWRENCE AND JACOB LAWRENCE

Gwendolyn Knight Lawrence, artist

Having been born in Barbados, I was not familiar with "Lift Every Voice and Sing" during my earliest childhood. My family moved to Harlem just as I entered my teen years and, as Episcopalians, we affiliated with St. Philip's Episcopal Church, where Father Bishop was pastor. But I became much more aware of the song during the early 1960s, as black people in Harlem and across the nation began to intensify and solidify their commitment to the demand for their civil rights and the various related movements.

It was very moving to find yourself in a massive audience of hundreds or even thousands and have them rise about you as one body when the introductory strands of the song were played. The music was so compelling! Then, as their voices were lifted in song, the words seemed to be their *very own* and were uplifting, powerful, and strong.

Whenever and wherever I have heard "Lift Every Voice and Sing," it seemed to express an outpouring of determination and confidence that justice could and would be achieved. My husband's depiction of the song expresses this so clearly.

Jacob Lawrence, artist

I never met James Weldon Johnson but I do recall my first memory of hearing "Lift Every Voice and Sing." It was during the early

Jacob Lawrence

1930s, at the Abyssinian Baptist Church in Harlem when the Reverend Adam Clayton Powell, Sr., was pastor. The words of the hymn seemed to express so well the expectation felt by black people everywhere—it is my opinion that they touch the soul and spirit of all who hear them.

I was spurred by the music written by James Weldon's brother, Rosamond, and the import of his poetry made the creation of the painting [see page 163] a most joyful experience for me.

The vertical composition of the drawing represents the ongoing climb toward Liberty, while the broad bare feet of the figure at the bottom signify "the steady beat" of "weary feet." The flower and the leaf in the hands of two of the figures denote life and "the hope that the present has brought us." The sun shining out of the upper left-hand corner symbolizes "our new day begun."

One has only to find himself standing in the midst of a large congregation of African Americans (as I found myself on that Sunday morning in the 1930s) singing this inspiring hymn to feel its great power and strong spiritual appeal.

# NORMAN LEAR

television executive and producer

I found myself clapping and swaying at the New Shiloh Baptist Church in Baltimore to the rhythms of "Lift Every Voice and Sing" on a cool spring evening in 1997. In a collaborative campaign of People for the American Way and the local chapter of the NAACP, we had spent the day rallying against a proposed voucher program for the Baltimore public schools.

Now, in that packed church, amidst ecstatic cries and swooping gospel singing, the evening finale of "Lift Every Voice" brought the day into focus: "Lift every voice and sing / Till earth and heaven ring."

This great hymn of freedom gave us a way to celebrate past victories, humbly call for strength in the challenges facing us, and

*Dancing at the Cotillion Society Ball, c. 1960s.* Photograph by John W. Mosley, courtesy of The Charles L. Blockson Afro-American Collection, Temple University.

make a bold declaration of faith in the ultimate triumph of good. Was that a whoop of "Hallelujah!" that irrepressibly burst forth from my overflowing heart?

I have recalled that evening on many occasions. It conjured up similar evenings, in the 1960s, when I first learned the hymn from black colleagues and activists. I was greatly moved by its emotional power then.

Now, another generation of young organizers and activists is being inducted into a great intergenerational community. The strands of spirit that connect this vast community across one hundred years involve faith and a shared struggle for justice. They involve our simple humanity and quest for beloved community.

Could there be a greater need for such virtues than at a time when affirmative action and the Confederate flag are the center of awful political spectacles? When minority voices remain rare on prime-time television and racial tensions divide college campuses?

That is precisely why I have been fortified by "Lift Every Voice." The hymn acknowledges tragedy and struggle while affirming hope and renewal. It exemplifies the spirit with which People for the American Way now collaborates with the NAACP in the Partners for Public Education project. Working with Kweisi Mfume, NAACP president and CEO, PFAW is organizing parents and students to stand up for stronger public schools and fight proposals that would weaken or destroy them.

I have felt—we all feel—immense spiritual power when black and white Americans struggle together toward a common vision of social justice—"the harmonies of Liberty." Our singing of "Lift Every Voice" proclaims this joyous truth.

# EDWARD LEWIS

publisher, *Essence* magazine

I believe there has never been a song, or any writing, that has so vividly captured the struggles, hopes, and dreams of a people. Fondly known as the Negro National Anthem, "Lift Every Voice and Sing" is a song of praise, a song of hope, an anthem for all people—and arguably the greatest testimony to the African American experience. A testimony that God is always with you, even in the darkest hour. A testimony to an ongoing struggle for freedom, justice, and equality.

This great song tells of independence, atonement, and self-determination. It speaks to the best of what we were, what we are, and what—with God's help—we ever hope to become.

As we enter a new age—a new millennium—we all will face new challenges and enjoy new opportunities. How we come together as a community to take advantage of those opportunities and find solutions to those challenges will be our testimony to the writers of "Lift Every Voice and Sing" and to the others who came before us. "Out from the gloomy past, / Till now we stand at last / Where the white gleam of our bright star is cast."

Let us remember the words of this great song and be inspired. Let us stay connected to each other and to "our native land." And "may we forever stand" together and sing this magnificent declaration of hope for a better tomorrow and a brighter future.

# LILLIAN AND JOHN LEWIS

Lillian Lewis, official, Clark Atlanta University

Mrs. Nellie Brewster Render, a native of North Carolina, my second-grade teacher at the Forty-ninth Street Elementary School in Los Angeles, introduced me to "Lift Every Voice and Sing" in 1947. Mrs. Render had a way of changing her demeanor depending on

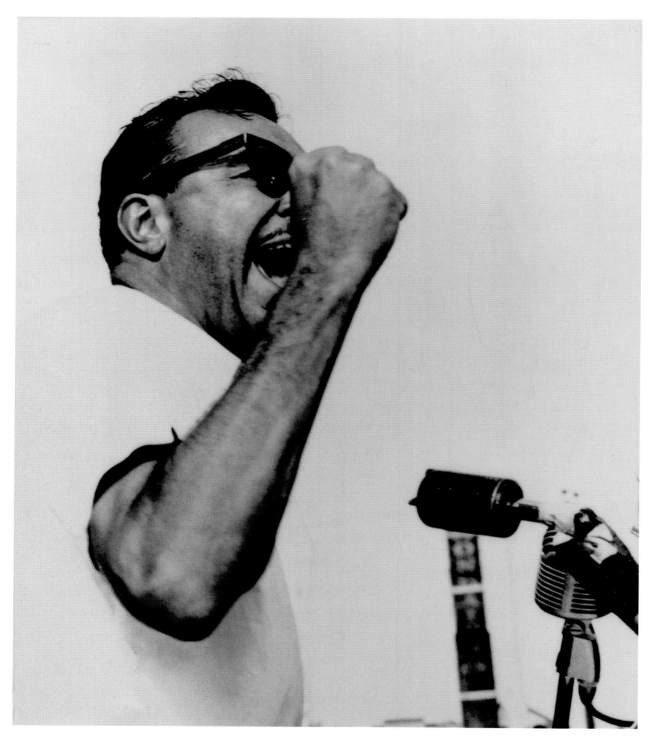

*Adam Clayton Powell, Jr., speaks at a civil rights rally in Atlantic City, 1964.* Photograph by John W. Mosley, courtesy of The Charles L. Blockson Collection, Temple University

what she wanted from her students. We second-graders knew when she was serious, and we understood when she was in a cheerful mood. One morning she stood erect and looked from one student to another. Observing her sedate comportment, we understood that we were to keep quiet and pay close attention to what she was about to tell us. "What I am about to write on the blackboard will stay with you students for the rest of your lives," she said. And so Mrs. Render proceeded to write the three stanzas of "Lift Every Voice and Sing." As she wrote, one could have heard a pin drop in the class; our eyes were glued to the blackboard, capturing her every word. After we copied the stanzas, Mrs. Render taught us the song by what she called a pitch round. This meant that she sang a line, then we sang the same line, until all the lines were sung. When she finally played the music on the piano, "Lift Every Voice and Sing" came to life for me.

Today, when I think of patriotic songs, "America" is very special to me. But I place "Lift Every Voice and Sing" right beside it. They both pull the strings of my heart.

After one hundred years, the truth of "Lift Every Voice and Sing" still marches on.

John Lewis, U.S. representative, Georgia

I grew up in rural southeast Alabama. In those years, we celebrated Negro History Week during February. My fourth-grade teacher asked each student to prepare a scrapbook to celebrate Negro History Week. To commence this assignment, I searched through magazines like *Opportunity* and *The Crisis* and our local newspapers. I filled my scrapbook with Paul Laurence Dunbar's pictures and poems; writings on or by Frederick Douglass; and Underground Railroad stories about Harriet Tubman. I also came across a poem: "Lift Every Voice and Sing." In my nine-year-old mind, my reason for clipping the three stanzas was twofold: I liked the way it read, and it was written by a black man. I didn't, however, understand in those early years what the words would one day mean to me and black America.

*Young dancers before a performance, c. 1960s.* Photograph by John W. Mosley, courtesy of The Charles L. Blockson Afro-American Collection, Temple University

Years later, while a student at American Baptist Theological College, I joined an NAACP local branch. Dr. Martin Luther King, Jr., Thurgood Marshall, Roy Wilkins, and other important black leaders of the day came to our branch as guest speakers for rallies or other events. "Lift Every Voice" was always sung following these uplifting and informative gatherings. As I reflect on those years, even before I knew that the song was considered the Negro National Anthem, I can't remember anyone telling me to stand while singing it. I never asked why we stood. I simply knew intuitively that it was revered and held sacred by black Americans.

During the turbulent 1960s when both black and white freedom fighters were clubbed, cursed, and murdered fighting for a race's liberation, songs like "Lift Every Voice and Sing" fortified the civil rights movement with their spiritual essence, fostering the momentum that we so desperately needed to continue the struggle. Without the Negro National Anthem and certain other songs, the civil rights movement would have been like a bird without wings.

My prayer and hope for this nation in this new century is that we will all come together as Americans, tear down the heavy burden of race prejudice, and create one house—one family—the American family.

## LEON LITWACK

history professor, University of California, Berkeley

Although written at the height of racist terror in the South, James Weldon Johnson's "Lift Every Voice and Sing" addressed the new century with optimism and hope.

> *Sing a song full of the faith that the dark past has taught us,*
> *Sing a song full of the hope that the present has brought us:*
> *Facing the rising sun of our new day begun,*
> *Let us march on till victory is won.*

*Dr. Betty Shabazz makes a point with an unidentified man (note the photograph of Malcolm X on the wall), late 1960s.*

Courtesy of Gamilah-L. Shabazz

Three years later, in *The Souls of Black Folk,* W. E. B. Du Bois offered a more sobering assessment: "The problem of the twentieth century is the problem of the color-line." Less optimistic than Johnson, he envisaged a painful and unrelenting struggle waged by a beleaguered people, many of whom had already become interior exiles, disenfranchised, victims of crushed hopes, stifled ambition, and betrayed expectations. "And all this life and love and strife and failure," Du Bois reflected, "is it the twilight of nightfall or the flush of some faint-dawning day?"

From James Weldon Johnson's "Lift Every Voice and Sing" to "We Shall Overcome" to Sam Cooke's "A Change Is Gonna Come," black Americans gave voice to a confident faith in progress and in their ability to undermine the vestiges of white supremacy and racism. But the victory envisioned in Johnson's anthem and by the civil rights movement remains elusive. Slavery and Jim Crow have been abolished, but we continue to live with their legacy—in our racial attitudes, in our institutions, in our police and judicial practices, in the extent of the racial divide. No matter how it is measured—by where most blacks live, by the jobs they hold, by their income, by the schools they attend, or by their future prospects—the United States remains in critical ways two societies, separate and unequal, and racism remains the most crippling virus in the American system, capable of assuming different guises as the occasion requires. Genuine equality demands a restructuring of society that most Americans are unwilling to accept, including equal access to economic and educational resources and political power, and a fundamental redistribution of wealth and income.

Some forty years after the civil rights movement peaked, a new generation of black Americans is less confident about its prospects, having experienced a serious erosion of the national commitment to civil rights. "Lift Every Voice and Sing" would find little resonance (even recognition) among young blacks listening to Snoop Doggy Dogg, NWA (Niggaz With Attitude), Outkast, the Geto Boys, Urban Underground, Tupac Shakur, Lady of Rage, and ODB (Ol' Dirty Bastard). Perhaps with Sam Cooke in mind, WC & the MAAD Circle rapped, "Yeah, it's 1997 y'all and ain't a damn thing changed." Declaring themselves "Rebels Without a Pause," Public Enemy admonished young blacks to "fight the power," and "Don't, don't, don't believe the hype."

James Weldon Johnson's "Lift Every Voice and Sing," or Public Enemy's "Fight the Power": who is to say which voice comes closer to capturing the tough reality that still resonates in much of black America as we enter the twenty-first century?

# MICHAEL L. LOMAX

president, Dillard University

James Weldon Johnson is best known today as a literary artist. *The Autobiography of an Ex-Colored Man* and *God's Trombones* are classics of the African American canon. His poetry remains popular among contemporary readers. Hardly an oratorical or amateur dramatic presentation in the black community today is complete without a rendering of Johnson's verse sermons. Their power and unpretentious eloquence are testaments to the traditions of black preaching and to Johnson's abiding respect for these spiritual messengers and their unique voice. Like the preachers themselves, Johnson combined the language of the King James Bible with images and diction drawn from everyday life. "Lift Every Voice and Sing" has become the universally acknowledged Negro National Anthem, I suspect, because it captures the heroic themes of black life in the language of the Bible and the traditional Negro spirituals. Pain and promise, struggle and hard-won accomplishments, difficulty met with determination, faith, and the expectation of a new day—these are the powerful truths of black life, and Johnson has captured them so clearly that the work he and his brother Rosamond composed to celebrate Lincoln's birthday in 1900 remains remarkably current at the dawn of yet another century.

I am frustrated that harmony in race relations remains the unfulfilled promise of the world's most powerful democracy. Certainly, I have witnessed in my lifetime the removal of barriers and the

*"I want to go to collage too," c. 1960s.* Photograph by John W. Mosley, courtesy of The Charles L. Blockson Afro-American Collection, Temple University

passage of laws, the fruits of hard-fought battles and persistent agitation. In particular, I now travel the South with a sense of fearlessness and freedom that I could not have imagined four decades ago. I know that I have seen seismic changes in American society—yet we have not achieved all that we should, and for too many of my brothers and sisters the color of their skin is still more important than the content of their character. For all our progress, too many African Americans remain on the margins, excluded from full participation in American life and the bounties that have been the birthright of so many other citizens.

Given the work yet to be done, Johnson's words remain an apt anthem for the century ahead: "Facing the rising sun of our new day begun / Let us march on till victory is won." Like the weekly messages in our churches, like the words of the "black and unknown bards" who composed our spirituals, Johnson's anthem captures my sense of the past, the present, and the future. Our struggles have brought us to our present plateau but we are still on our journey. In a sense, this is the journey of all humankind: the pilgrimage toward the ideal. Johnson's poetry tells the story of a people, but it also expresses the aspirations of all people who travel the difficult road from slavery to freedom. To the extent that there can be a universal message in any particular people's history, Johnson has articulated one here. These words and themes resonate, I suspect, for all people struggling to shake off the manacles of bondage. Just as I am no longer surprised to hear people all around the world sing "We Shall Overcome," I would not be surprised in my lifetime to hear Johnson's powerful words serve as the anthem for other people who, like black Americans, are on the freedom journey and thus find in "Lift Every Voice and Sing" the same beauty and inspiration that we have found for the last one hundred years.

*Eubie Blake (seated) and Billy Taylor, jazz pianists and composers, 1970s.* Courtesy of Schomburg Center for Research in Black Culture, The New York Public Library

# FRANK MEEKS

president, Domino's Pizza, Team Washington

James Weldon Johnson's turn-of-the-century Negro anthem, "Lift Every Voice and Sing," speaks directly and potently to the spirit of life, the spirit of music, the spirit of God. And this Spirit—Faith in God and in sustaining families—was the better part of their survival for many turn-of-the-century blacks. The song immediately recalls the Jim Crow era, in which the spirit and dreams of black youths were twisted inward by white oppression. It recalls a time when those who railed against their oppressors were left crumpled and lifeless on the ground.

In the century since Johnson first penned "Lift Every Voice," the problems associated with skin pigmentation in this country have improved. In some ways, though, they may have gotten worse. Consider that racism today is far subtler than it was in the days when KKK members regularly stomped down streets with sheets over their heads, spewing vitriolic rage. At least you could see that sort of racism coming a mile away. Racism now manifests itself in the cultural patterns that a shared history of slavery and racism wrought. It is about a cultural division that was sewn so deeply into our social fabric, for so long, that the social hierarchies it established continue to influence us.

In short, today's racism is largely economic, a hangover from a time when blacks were valued only as cheap labor in this country. This sort of racism is potentially more dangerous because although we brush against it, we can't always see it. All the while it erodes not with a thunderous bang, but with the silent fury of a river current.

For this reason, "Lift Every Voice" continues to resonate in our hearts. It transcends the historical moment that created it, and it speaks to an eternal struggle: the fact that, in the words of Albert Camus, "we are condemned to live together."

For me, "Lift Every Voice" speaks to the need for corporate America to create jobs and invest in poor black neighborhoods.

*C. Delores Tucker sworn in as secretary of state of the Commonwealth of Pennsylvania by Judge A. Leon Higginbotham, 1974.* Photograph by John W. Mosley, courtesy of The Charles L. Blockson Afro-American Collection, Temple University

One of the most satisfying things for me is to take a high-school-age inner-city youth who could very easily be on the streets learning the drug trade, and teach him what it takes to own his own business, endow him with the expectation of other possibilities.

To "lift every voice" means to change the economic hierarchies by lifting up a hand and creating jobs for black America in black American neighborhoods. Unfortunately, too many Americans quiver at the notion of driving into those neighborhoods, let alone investing in them. That is why it is so important that the government get serious about offering tax incentives for businesses to create jobs and opportunities there. Right now that same tax money is being used to provide welfare, with the effect of subsidizing idleness instead of subsidizing opportunity. Little will change in the new millennium until corporate America steps up to the plate, goes into these neighborhoods, and creates opportunity.

By altering the economic complexion of our inner cities, we can alter the complexion of race relations. Progress, in this regard, will turn largely upon the friction of honest people working together to create jobs and role models for young blacks in the inner city.

# CONSTANCE BAKER MOTLEY

federal judge

"Lift Every Voice and Sing," a song about the dark past of a race and its glorious possibilities, speaks so passionately of the twentieth century's black struggle. The Johnson brothers' song became a musical sanctum for a people seeking liberation at a time when we African Americans desperately needed a message of faith and there was little on which to rest that faith. Throughout the arduous years of the black struggle, "Lift Every Voice and Sing," vocalized in churches, schools, civic auditoriums—wherever black people gathered for the cause of freedom—inspired us to move forward.

"Lift Every Voice and Sing" was written four years after the Supreme Court decision in *Plessy v. Ferguson* (1896). In *Plessy*, a preponderance of the justices gave their resolute ratification to a "separate but equal" doctrine. The reality behind *Plessy* was that an overwhelming majority of whites, particularly in the South, refused to accept black Americans as equals in American society; the Supreme Court's decision was a newer interpretation of the Equal Protection requirements of the Fourteenth Amendment, which was then only twenty-eight years old. While denying racism on the one hand, the *Plessy* decision reaffirmed it on the other. Only Justice John Marshall Harlan, in his lone dissent, acknowledged this racist affirmation and correctly predicted its corrosive effect on twentieth-century American society. In response to the High Court's ruling, African Americans have spent the twentieth century battling racism. We African Americans took James Weldon Johnson's words "Let us march on till victory is won" to heart and head as we battled for justice and were victorious in the Supreme Court's *Brown* decision—our twentieth-century civil rights legacy. The *Brown* decision construed the equal-protection clause of the Fourteenth Amendment as barring any racial distinctions by a state government as well as the federal government, because of the due-process clause of the Fifth Amendment. And, as a result of that 1954 decision and its progeny, official racism, once again, has been constitutionally barred. After *Brown,* what remained largely unrestrained was private racism—a form of racism that continues to be unconquered.

We ended the twentieth century with the recognition that racism, a problem we should have resolved with strong and consistent national leadership, is still with us. The question, therefore, is clear: what do we do about it? The answer can be found only in the history of what we have done about racism in the past century. James Weldon Johnson's line "Sing a song full of the faith that the dark past has taught us" poignantly embodies this sentiment.

*Yvonne Benjamin and Charles Adams, 1974.* Courtesy of Yvonne Benjamin

# ALBERT MURRAY

scholar, critic, and author

When I was invited to write an essay on "Lift Every Voice and Sing" for its centennial, I decided to quote from a book I wrote some years back: *South to a Very Old Place.* I cannot say it better.

You look for the old landmarks along Peachtree Street (including Zachary and Muse's the haberdashers which were to the Atlanta of your Tuskegee days what Fanin's was to Montgomery and Metzger's was to Mobile). Then you make your way once more to Rich's bookstore, remembering how it was when you first saw it back during the heyday of *Gone With the Wind,* which was also when Atlanta was trying to be an even older place than it was before the Sherman caper, saying gone with the wind but trying like hell to look as far as possible back beyond the so-called New South of Henry W. Grady all the same.

Then from Rich's you take the bus out to West Hunter to see Atlanta University, Morehouse, Spelman, Clark, and Morris Brown once more, remembering how the fried chicken in Ma Sutton's café used to be worth the trip in spite of the fact that the reason you used to make it was that the downtown Atlanta of those days was so goddam segregated you couldn't even use a clean rest room; remembering also that Atlanta University had also been a part of the so-called New South and that one of its finest graduates was James Weldon Johnson of the class of 1894 and that W. E. B. Du Bois during his first period there (1896–1909) had written *The Souls of Black Folk* and had also initiated, according to Guy B. Johnson, the first real sociological research in the South.

You also remember how during your days at Mobile County Training School the rotogravure sepia images of Du Bois in his satanic goatee, Booker T. Washington (close-cropped, beardless, full-lipped, and without mustache), Frederick Douglass (coin-perfect in his lion's mane), Harriet Tubman in her glorious bandanna, old knob-headed Jack Johnson with his satin-smooth shoulders and tight pants, and all the rest of them used to blend together in a

*Roy Wilkins, executive director of the NAACP, 1970s.* Courtesy of Mildred Bond Roxborough

sepia-bronze panorama when the student body used to stand and sing "Lift Every Voice and Sing," which was written by that same golden brown James Weldon Johnson and his brother J. Rosamond Johnson and which everybody used to call the Negro National Anthem—but which for you was first of all the Brown American nation school bell anthem (the comb your hair brush your teeth shine your shoes crease your trousers tie your tie clean your nails rub a dub stand sit and look straight make folks proud anthem!). So far as you are concerned, not even Martin Luther King—the stamping ground of whose youngmanhood you are treading even now—could inspire his most eager followers to put as much aspiration and determination into "We Shall Overcome" as people always used to get into James Weldon Johnson and J. Rosamond Johnson's school bell song.

## JESSYE NORMAN

opera singer

First of all, it is a mighty anthem; highly singable, stirring, and satisfying. When I was a youngster in Augusta, Georgia, it was one of the main parts of the Emancipation Proclamation Celebration each year on January 1 at the city's largest black church, Tabernacle Baptist. Each of these services ended with this song. The church is a magnificent structure . . . red brick with white stucco trim outside, with a sanctuary the shape of a rather good concert hall. It was always a place of drama and grandeur. The important meetings and conferences of the NAACP were always held there. It was the church, of course, where Dr. Martin Luther King, Jr., spoke when he visited Augusta. It was a fitting setting for a child to experience this song for the first time.

I have always marveled at the eloquence and depth of the words, so full of pathos but with the underpinning of hope that recalls the *light* in the most moving of spirituals. Through the darkness, through the heart-wrenching present, hope abides. "Lift

Every Voice" speaks to the age-old need to give voice to one's deepest sorrows and longings; a determination to believe in a better tomorrow even when optimism is a challenge for the mind to embrace.

In the spring of 1999, when I was asked to sing in the Rotunda of the U.S. Capitol for the congressional ceremony honoring Rosa Parks, I was happy to find that even though I had not sung this wonderful song in a while, all of the verses were still somewhere in my memory. It was a moment to remember. Many people joined with me in that performance, and many knew all of the words, including the President! I was moved beyond words.

The Johnson brothers have left much that constitutes their legacy, but I would guess that "Lift Every Voice and Sing" will remain for all time as perhaps the most meaningful and lasting of their contributions to our rich and varied history.

# CHARLES J. OGLETREE, JR.

law professor, Harvard University

When I sing the American National Anthem, I do so out of respect for the patriots who fought against oppression from a foreign land. When I recite the Pledge of Allegiance, it reminds me of a nation committed to defending its soil against all hostile intruders and focused on freedom and equality.

When I sing James Weldon Johnson's Negro National Anthem, I feel a deeper and more emotional attachment. First and foremost, it is a vivid reminder of the suffering of millions of slaves who were brought to a foreign land against their will. Moreover, it provides a powerful illustration of the deep riches of Africa and its profound impact on our society and values. The Negro National Anthem reminds me that the postmodern view of "family values" does not fully encompass the African concept of community. The African proverb "It takes a village to raise a child" offers a deep appreciation of the values of community, unity, and teamwork that is often lack-

*Sammy Davis, Jr., star of the* NBC Follies, *1973.* Courtesy of Schomburg Center for Research in Black Culture, The New York Public Library

ing in other societies. Moreover, the Negro National Anthem reminds me of the incredible resilience that African Americans must have so as to endure slavery, Jim Crow laws, lynchings, and intolerance on the part of many individuals and institutions in this country. It reminds me of how far we've come, even though the path has been difficult and often treacherous. It reminds me of how far we need to go, and how important it will be for all of us to join in the effort to realize the dreams that James Weldon Johnson so eloquently described. It also reminds me of the value of unity without discord, dissension, or division, the truly African American principle that needs to be shared by all nations and people.

It reminds me that we can never forget the pain that the voiceless and faceless slaves endured, and that it is our obligation to forever raise our voices in opposition to any effort that seeks to obstruct progress for the reluctant visitors to this land. Finally, it reminds me that, unlike some songs that have a time and a place, the Negro National Anthem is timeless and has no borders. It is a true reflection of a remarkable people surviving under the most difficult of circumstances with a vision that is all-encompassing and spiritually inspired, with hope as the key ingredient. It is a song for all times, for all seasons, and for all people.

## OLLIE JEWEL SIMS OKALA

retired public-health nurse

This tribute to the centennial of "Lift Every Voice and Sing" is a profoundly moving moment in my life. Having been privileged and blessed to live in the home of Mr. and Mrs. James Weldon Johnson and be accepted as a member of their family, I am honored to write about what "Lift Every Voice and Sing" means to me.

Writing this essay takes me back to my years as a nursing student at Meharry Medical College in Nashville during the early 1930s. I was moved to tears when I first heard the Fisk Jubilee Singers present "Lift Every Voice and Sing." Listening to this

*"The Demagogic Politician Is Not to Be Left Out in This Case"*: *A member of the Black Panther party displaying a copy of* The Black Panther *newspaper, 1970s.* Courtesy of Schomburg Center for Research in Black Culture, The New York Public Library

world-renowned choir, I was assailed by dual emotions—pride and sadness. My pride emanated from the fact that two African American men had given our race a song about hope and dreams. At a time when black Americans were considered unworthy to be American citizens, James Weldon Johnson told us in "Lift Every Voice and Sing" that we do have it in us to be the best that we can be. My sadness stemmed from the grim life I had lived as a young child in North Little Rock, Arkansas. This bleakness grew out of the harsh racism and abject poverty that I endured in the early years of my life—a kind of poverty and racism that no child in this rich land should have to bear.

James Weldon Johnson called "Lift Every Voice and Sing" his and Rosamond's "Hymn." He and I frequently talked about the song, usually after I had heard a particular choir perform it. I eagerly related to him how the choir sang the song; or how the audience reacted with pride; or how the chorus "brought down the house" singing his "anthem." In his typical calm manner, he never failed to remind me that "a nation can have but one anthem and our anthem is 'The Star-Spangled Banner.'" He nevertheless fully understood the inequitable conditions in America that moved his race to embrace "Lift Every Voice and Sing" as an anthem of heart and soul.

The serenity that flows from the song gave me solace on the day Mrs. James Weldon Johnson died, November 1, 1976. Earlier that year, on July 24, she had suffered a stroke that rendered her voiceless. Accordingly Grace Nail Johnson and I established a method of communication. For example, when I asked a question, if her response was yes, she blinked once; if her response was no, she blinked twice. The memory of the glistening sunlight that overlaid her bedroom on the day she died remains vivid in my mind. And in the midst of this sun-filled setting, it became evident to me, a registered nurse, that her death was imminent. I needed to make these last moments of her life special ones. Suddenly the answer occurred to me. "Do you want me to play 'Lift Every Voice and Sing'?" I asked. Her eyes showed a sparkle before she blinked once and nodded yes. I put the record on our old record player. She leaned back against her pillow, appearing contented and relaxed as her mind absorbed the words her husband had written seventy-six years earlier: "God of our weary years, God of our silent tears, / Thou who hast brought us thus far on the way . . ." While the song played, I leaned downward and whispered, "Grace, I will do everything humanly possible to keep James Weldon Johnson's memory alive. Do you understand?" She blinked once. Minutes later, Mrs. James Weldon Johnson was gone.

As this new century evolves I, like James Weldon Johnson, believe "Lift Every Voice and Sing" should be sung around the world with appreciation. The line "Sing a song full of the hope that the present has brought us" assuredly resonates universally.

# Gordon Parks

photographer, filmmaker, author

"Lift Every Voice and Sing" soars from the depths of our history. The lyrics, mothering and cradling, forcefully reject those dark years that fed our suffering. Free now of their mournful light, our hopes shimmer through the music like stars. Coming to grips with past sorrows, the anthem raises a relentless fist against despair, while warning us that living on hope alone can be akin to living on air and smoke. It urges us to keep moving on until equality and freedom surround us with the oneness of the sky.

After surviving a host of angry solitudes, many black people were still looking bitterly toward white silence when James Weldon Johnson and J. Rosamond Johnson put our anthem to words and music. Bigotry was spreading like wildfire then. Mongers of racial hatred were beating their drums overtime when, in their own particular poetry, these brothers lifted our voices to ring over earth and heaven. In doing so they found the flavor of our hopes and prayers, then brought them together to face the onslaught of more violent

*Karl Hampton Porter, bassoonist, music educator, and conductor, who organized one of the nation's first multi-ethnic symphony orchestras, 1971.* Courtesy of Evelyn Barnes Parker

days. Having caught the smell of our dreams, the music and lyrics kept swelling, kept sinking deep into our hearts—so deeply that even time fails to wipe out their existence.

But it took time, brutal time, for us arrive at the gates of resistance and say good-bye to fear. Even in this year of 2000, fear still stands tapping its foot, waiting for us to come back and bow to it. It should know by now that we will never return to its ravages. Though crushed and burned, it still waits. Blinded by the odds that confront our blackness, it fails to realize that the volcano of black blood flowing through those bitter years washed out its footprints.

So we walk on and on, asking indiscreet questions, but yielding only to those answers that sing of equality and freedom. Only an honorable existence can purify our intentions. If bigots decide to talk with us, they must speak our language. If they find that too difficult, let them have a conversation with our past—then be gone in a hurry.

As a race we lived too long without actually living. How many of our ancestors perished on the way to our rebirth? How dearly must we keep paying to live on this planet? In response to these questions a multitude of voices remain silent. But the questions refuse to die. Our roots are talking with history, and history still holds the bitter smell of our lifetime of turbulence. Its bell still tolls to the sound of our dead. No longer can we be content to just ask questions, then die. Better we live on to fight new fires that flame up to disrupt our dreams.

# COLIN L. POWELL

former chairman, Joint Chiefs of Staff

I especially enjoy "Lift Every Voice and Sing" when it follows the National Anthem. Together, both anthems capture the struggle of black Americans for equality. The National Anthem speaks of the promise of America and our willingness to fight and to die to remain the "land of the free." "The Star-Spangled Banner" is a sym-

*President Jimmy Carter meeting with presidents of historically black colleges and universities at the White House, late 1970s.* Courtesy of Schomburg Center for Research in Black Culture, The New York Public Library

bol of that freedom, a freedom given to all men and women by God and secured by government as called for in our Declaration of Independence, Constitution, and Bill of Rights. It represents an ideal that was promised, but not granted to all.

"Lift Every Voice" sings of the crusade black Americans fought to gain the blessings of freedom. It is a yearning, poignant hymn of hope, suffering, and aspiration that arises from the depth of despair. It is a triumphant anthem soaring upward—"High as the listening skies, . . . Facing the rising sun. . . . Where the white gleam of our bright star is cast." Every stanza ends on a plateau of optimism where victory awaits. Its words have sustained us and given us strength for a hundred years, and will continue to do so for years to come.

"The Star-Spangled Banner" is the promise. Without that promise, the struggle chronicled in "Lift Every Voice" would have no goal to reach. Together, the promise and reality grow closer and closer, leading to that day when the dream will be fulfilled.

# HUGH B. PRICE

president and CEO, National Urban League

> *Lift every voice and sing*
> *Till earth and heaven ring,*
> *Ring with the harmonies of Liberty . . .*

In the early twentieth century, when James Weldon Johnson and his brother, J. Rosamond Johnson, composed the music and the lyrics to our anthem, what did Liberty mean to black Americans?

For until then, throughout their entire existence on the North American continent, people of African descent had never been free, not as white colonists from England and Europe had sought to be free when they fled the Old World to settle in the New. Certainly not free as "freedom" was defined by the rebels who in the 1770s and 1780s waged a war to establish the United States of America.

"We hold these Truths to be self-evident; that all Men are created equal," they wrote—and then defined black men, women, and children as less than human, as worth only three-fifths of a white man. Even the "freedom" of the black people of this time who had either escaped from or not been born into slavery was something considerably less than that enjoyed by white Americans.

In those early decades, in those centuries, it took extraordinary courage for people of African descent to declare that they, too, deserved Liberty, and that they intended to seek it.

That high level of courage was still necessary when "Lift Every Voice" was composed. Segregation was entrenched by law in the South, and by rigid custom which had the force of law in the North and West. These twin forces of racism combined to hem African Americans in to a very small corner of American life, a small corner with high walls.

Yet black Americans like James Weldon and J. Rosamond Johnson were looking beyond the boundaries, exerting themselves to live the lives of free men and women. They were full of the faith and full of the hope that African Americans would ultimately triumph.

That is why they opened this anthem in such powerful fashion: "Lift every voice and sing" with such faith and hope and power as to make the heavens resound.

You might say the Johnson brothers were preaching to the choir. Let us not forget that church is still in session.

# PHYLICIA RASHAD

actress

As a second-grade student, I attended Paul Laurence Dunbar Elementary in Houston, Texas. In those days, Negro History Week was celebrated in February. It was during this time that my mother, Vivian Ayers, came to teach our class the Negro National Anthem.

*Singers Betty Carter (left) and Ella Fitzgerald (center) in lively conversation with the jazz trombonist and arranger Melba Liston, 1988.* Courtesy of Schomburg Center for Research in Black Culture, The New York Public Library

The *Negro* National Anthem—that had quite a ring to it. The Negro National Anthem—imagine that! We had our own anthem!

My mother was a brilliant pianist who played with her whole being. I had heard many musical compositions before, but never this one. She played with such vigor, strength, and purpose that we became filled with enthusiasm as well, carefully enunciating every syllable. We were a small group of second-graders, but when we sang in assembly that week, we felt as grand and as powerful as the Antioch Baptist Church Choir. The anthem was large, and we were large in it.

*Lift every voice and sing!*

The cadence alone conjured images of millions of souls long departed—all ancestors—marching to glory, urging on the future. It was exhilarating. We were singing for ourselves as well as for and with them. It made the hairs on my arms stand up.

*Stony the road we trod, bitter the chastening rod . . .*

As a seven-year-old, I didn't comprehend the mystery that lies within the lesson of these simple words. Truthfully speaking, I hesitate to claim complete understanding as an adult; however, I do realize that they, the words, are prophetic in nature. Humanity's struggle for "victory" has not yet ended—indeed, we seem far from it! Through the miracle of modern technology we are able to access and disseminate information to and from almost anywhere in this world at an ever-increasing speed—a feat unimaginable to most at the beginning of the twentieth century. Today we stand tall and proudly proclaim "improved communications"! However, respect for the dignity of all humankind, tolerance, understanding, forgiveness, and love are not matters of technology. They are attributes of the heart and character of the human being; instilled and nurtured by family and community. This is the foundation of communication among people.

*Muslim women worshiping in a mosque, c. 1980s.* Photograph by Ernie Paniccioli

*Lest our hearts, drunk with the wine of the world, we forget*
  *Thee;*
*Shadowed beneath Thy hand,*
*May we forever stand . . .*

Even in childhood it was obvious to me that remembrance of and faith in the Creator bonded people and bestowed courage and strength to face and overcome adversity. It is through reverence that we attain the experience of our highest Self and are compelled to fulfill our greatest duty—service to each other. I can't remember exactly when, but it occurred to me that the Negro National Anthem is the anthem of all humanity. James Weldon Johnson, the transcendent poet of this time, wrote from the vantage of what there is of the Creator within us all. This is how the truly human message is delivered.

## PAUL ROBESON, JR.

engineer and author

For me, the Negro National Anthem has always been a source of inspiration and inner strength. Today, as our struggle for equal opportunity as African American people continues into the twenty-first century, "Lift Every Voice and Sing" reminds me both of our distinctive culture, which successfully resisted the oppression of slavery and has sparked our progress since emancipation, and of the enormous obstacles we must still overcome in order to command fair treatment by American society. In celebrating Emancipation Day and the birthday of the Reverend Martin Luther King, Jr., it is appropriate to remind our callous nation that we as a people do not share the selfish, radical-individualist values of the popular culture, and will never accommodate to the present racially and economically biased status quo.

It is time to reassert our core values in every aspect of American life, since they are at the foundation of the humanistic thrust that

*A break dancer draws a crowd, 1980s.* Photograph by Ernie Paniccioli

is the world's only salvation in the coming millennium. Our value system demands commitment to the common good as well as pursuit of the highest achievement; it teaches respect for other cultures while nurturing one's own; it requires that gentleness and compassion accompany strength and power; it requires sacrifice to do what we know is right, instead of going along to get along. Above all, it rejects the idea that the individual is more important than the community; for us, the opposite is still true—the advancement of our people as a whole is more important than individual success.

Our future progress depends on our own unwavering commitment to our historical legacy in the face of the relentless efforts of the mass media to distort and manipulate it. Let us remember that Reverend King's "I Have a Dream" speech in 1963 contained a searing indictment of America's racist past and a warning that the "whirlwinds of revolt" would rock the nation "until the bright day of justice emerges." And let us pay heed to his 1967 admonition that racial justice cannot be separated from economic justice, and that structural changes in the system, rather than mere reforms, must be introduced. The past betrayal of the hopes of the vast majority of African Americans to provide limited gains for relatively few has dramatically confirmed King's prescience. The present rise of a powerful, racist right wing in American politics demands a revival of African American unity in a struggle more difficult than the civil rights revolution.

"Let us march on till victory is won."

## RACHEL ROBINSON

president, The Jackie Robinson Foundation

From the moment I first heard it as a small child at Bethel AME Church in Los Angeles to the present day, "Lift Every Voice and Sing" has echoed in my head and my heart as the anthem that straightens my back, lifts my head, and refreshes my spirit. It has helped me battle the temptation to yield to the despair, cynicism, and complacency that have always threatened to deter us African Americans from soldiering on and that remains endemic in our society. This song has helped me say again and again: I will not yield. For me it's been a rallying cry and a powerful weapon to combat the forces that threaten our progress.

The meaning of "Lift Every Voice" is what we at the Jackie Robinson Foundation have tried to do since our founding in 1973: give young people of color the help they need to pursue their dreams. From small beginnings, we now support more than two hundred Jackie Robinson Scholars a year at more than seventy colleges and universities with four-year scholarship awards that substantially address their financial needs. Equally important, our comprehensive support system, which prepares them for the world beyond college, has produced a 93 percent graduation rate among our students. This work with our young people, who are just entering adulthood and are flooded with questions about their identity and their future in America, is our way of obeying the charge of the song to "sing a song full of the faith" and "full of the hope" that come from the experience of being black in America. This faith and hope are among the qualities we try to instill in them. My awareness of their importance comes from this song of praise, which reminds us of the past and glorifies our struggles.

I know that we've made great progress in our struggle for unity, pride, and universal respect since "Lift Every Voice" was composed. But I also know that that progress in all areas has been slow, painfully achieved, and incomplete. "Lift Every Voice" reminds us to celebrate the advances, but be vigilant in devising new ways to use our institutions—this anthem being one of them—to create a new vanguard to meet the challenges of the present and the future.

*A gospel choir in performance, 1987.* Courtesy of Schomburg Center for Research in Black Culture, The New York Public Library

# DAVID ROCKEFELLER, JR.

chairman, Rockefeller Financial Services

As a soprano choirboy at ten and now as a bass chorister nearing sixty, I have been deeply touched by the power of simple, strong words set to beautiful music. "Lift Every Voice and Sing" is such music for me, its triplets rolling into long, sturdy downbeats whose very spaciousness ("voice . . . and . . . sing . . .") suggests there are words still to be written.

And indeed there *are* words still to be written in America's stammering history of racial division and racial healing. There is so much for us to do, but the Johnsons' stirring hymn prompts us to celebrate our successes, to remember the struggles, and to never lose hope for better times.

Music such as this has motivated me to spend decades of my life stretching across the cultural chasm of racial difference. Others have reached toward me and, more often now than before, our fingers seem to touch.

These moments—sometimes these long moments—come most often when we of different races are working together at something important. For example, in rehearsing Donald Sur's *Slavery Documents* and performing it in Boston's Symphony Hall with rows and rows of black and white listeners facing our blended Cantata Singers chorus on stage, all of us were torn apart and then reassembled by strong, simple words set to beautiful music.

I have also been privileged to work closely with an African American support group, the Friends of Education, at the Museum of Modern Art (MoMA) in New York City. Together we have examined MoMA's curatorial policies, its membership policies, and the museum's relationship with local schoolchildren. We have acknowledged our own racial chasms—existing even among sophisticated professionals—and we are committed to reaching across them and to learning from one another.

My work with Recruiting New Teachers, Inc., has also taught me a great deal about the educational needs of America's children.

RNT focuses on building a diverse teacher workforce for America's schools, particularly its urban schools. If America's classrooms are the petri dish for its adult society, we must surely address this matter of differences by helping all of our children to appreciate all of our citizens. Only then will we be able to proclaim that every voice has been lifted.

I thank the Johnson brothers for giving America a song of hope. I shall not forget it.

## VICTORIA ROWELL

actress

I was born and bred in Maine. Although there was just a smattering of African Americans in the Vacationland state, we had a strong sense of ourselves and our traditions; we had our land and we had God. We stood united, undeterred by whispers or flagrant racial slurs.

In the 1940s, my foster mother, Agatha C. Armstead (Wooten), purchased a sixty-acre farm with $2,000 she earned welding ships during World War II. It was not without a fight that she acquired her much beloved Forest's Edge. Various attempts to view the farm were denied. Agatha, originally from the Carolinas, had an indefatigable diligence about her. Finally, one of the owner's children allowed her into the house. Agatha knew immediately that this would be her home and went to the real estate office to purchase the farm.

Agatha C. Armstead was born in 1902, two generations removed from slavery. She was married and raised ten children during the Depression; nine survived. Her stories were painful and enlightening, they were happy and always wildly vivid. Receiving her amazing care gave me personal insight about my history as an African American.

I can remember sitting as a child with Agatha at an assembly for the desegregation of schools in Boston. Suddenly, everyone stood

*Muhammad Ali, 1980s.* Photograph by Chris Griffith

up and sang this glorious song . . . I'd never heard it before. My mother told me it was the Black National Anthem. A chorus of beautiful black voices resonating throughout the hall. One had to believe that God heard them.

Though Agatha Armstead began her life in a time of appalling civil injustices, she lived by the principle of God and family first. She was Light and represented victory in spite of perilous odds. Agatha Armstead is my "Lift Every Voice and Sing."

## MILDRED BOND ROXBOROUGH

former NAACP executive

I first learned about "Lift Every Voice and Sing" when I was about three or four years of age. Our parents, Ollie S. and Mattye T. Bond, regularly held reading sessions for my two older sisters while I was perched on the lap of the parent who held the session. My parents read from writings by Paul Laurence Dunbar, Frederick Douglass, John Greenleaf Whittier, Charles Waddell Chesnutt, Henry Wadsworth Longfellow, and others. My mother or father would offer a brief background on the author, then read a selection from their work. Afterward, we all discussed the reading.

It was during these years that my parents told us about James Weldon Johnson, whom they described as a man of many talents. They told us that he had written a passionate poem of prayer, "Lift Every Voice and Sing," in 1900 for "colored" children in Jacksonville, Florida. My parents read the poem-prayer frequently during these reading sessions.

By the age of six I was so impressed by this poem-prayer, I was moved to memorize it just as I had Longfellow's "Psalm of Life." The following year, I had begun reading *The Crisis* magazine. As subscribers, my parents frequently discussed the various articles in the journal with a serious urgency. I, therefore, understood the journal's significance to our lives as Americans of African descent.

I asked our parents for their consent to write Roy Wilkins, the

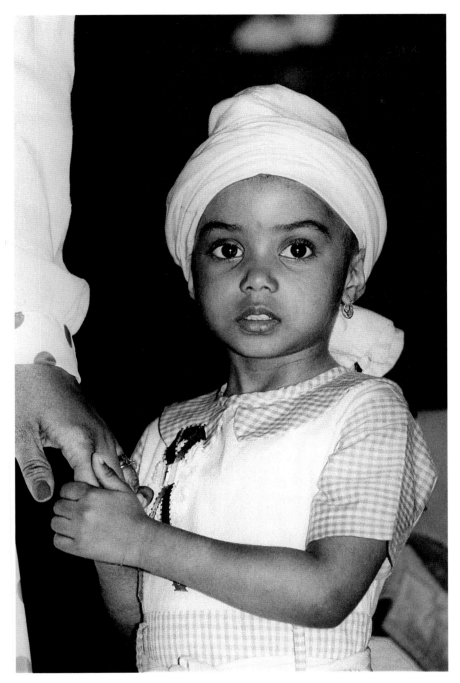

*A young girl clings to her mother's hand in church, 1980s.* Photograph by Chris Griffith

magazine's editor, to seek permission to sell copies in our community of Brownsville, Tennessee. When the first copies arrived, I read with varying degrees of comprehension. Imagine my joy and amazement when I came across my favorite poem-prayer, "Lift Every Voice and Sing," on a full page. As I went around our community selling *The Crisis,* my customers had to listen to a recitation of "Lift Every Voice and Sing." Subsequently, I would test them to determine if they had learned "our own hymn of prayer."

In June 1936, my parents received a charter for an NAACP branch in our town. At the special charter meeting, all members stood proudly and sang "Lift Every Voice and Sing." Afterward, many of them proclaimed to my parents that they had learned the words because they had been given no choice by me.

I joined the staff of the NAACP in 1954. I have been privileged to share the pathos, passion, and hope the song evokes in NAACP members for more than forty years. Whether I was involved in a workers' struggle for jobs in Key West, Florida, picketing for equal opportunity in the deep snow of Benton Harbor, Michigan, or working with the late Medgar Evers interviewing sharecroppers who suffered from economic reprisals, "Lift Every Voice and Sing" was like the ground beneath our feet that lifted us higher as we moved on to the next struggle.

In times of victory and tragedy, the NAACP family has gathered in countless cities, towns, and rural communities in this nation. There was never any doubt that we would rise on every occasion to sing our song of prayer. This remains an NAACP tradition.

"Lift Every Voice and Sing," the NAACP's official song, has been a source of inspiration and strength since my early childhood, when I was perched on the lap of either parent. It will always hold a treasured place in the storehouse of my memories and in my heart.

*On the dance floor, 1980s.* Photograph by Ernie Paniccioli

# SONIA SANCHEZ

poet, scholar, and author

I was born in Birmingham, Alabama. During my early school years, we sang "Lift Every Voice and Sing" at all weekly assemblies. The song was a school, church, and community ritual. I vividly remember Mr. Malicah Wilkinson, the music teacher at the Parker School in Birmingham, opening every event in town by saying, "Spread the word . . . lift every voice and sing." That meant everyone quickly rose and began singing.

My father found race prejudice in Birmingham intolerable in general, and particularly intolerable for himself as a musician. Even today he often recalls a frightening and confusing incident. He and other members of his band were invited by a white group to perform in a town about seventy miles from Birmingham. After they arrived at the park where they were to perform, they were thunderstruck by a large sign that hung at the entrance to the park: "Read nigger and run. And if you can't read, run anyhow." As he and the other band members stood there terrified, a white man yelled to my father, who was carrying his drums, "Boy, get on them drums and play."

It was this kind of blatant racism that caused my father to move our family to New York City. After arriving in New York, my sister and I attended Stitt Junior High School. During an assembly at Stitt, the entire student body was asked to sing the National Anthem. My sister and I stood, but we began to sing the only anthem we knew—"Lift Every Voice and Sing." Of course, we were the recipients of many stares and much wonderment—a very awkward moment for us at the time. But I know why I sang that anthem then, and why its power and beauty continue to be spiritual and inspiring.

# *Lift Every Voice and Sing: When I Sing You*

*When I sing you*
*You are sanctuary*
*A butterfly pausing in my blood;*
*When I sing you*
*I become holy knowing our grandmothers*
*Were the sermon James Weldon Johnson wrote about;*
*When I sing you*
*When I thread your words through my veins,*
*I become a river caressing our legs as we run for freedom;*
*When I hear your melody*
*I see our soft stone smiles,*
*We women and men coming out*
*Of the fire, shaking ourselves free;*
*When I swallow your words*
*I am at the beginning of our creation.*

## ILYASAH SHABAZZ

lecturer and municipal official

*Ilyasah (above) and Gamilah-L.
Shabazz*

Both of my parents, Malcolm X and Dr. Betty Shabazz, had great respect for world history, specifically African and American histories. When I was a small child, my mother took all of her six daughters to lectures, museums, any arena where we could learn history. Oftentimes, "Lift Every Voice and Sing" was sung at the onset of these events. When I was about eleven years old, I knew all three stanzas, and that certainly pleased my mother.

I'm always uplifted by the lyrics of the song because it soothed our spirits and still serves as a reminder of our ancestors and our historical experiences in America. It serves as a reminder of all of our contributions in spite of the inhuman conditions placed upon us.

*Chuck D at the Rap Against Racism rally, Harlem, 1989.* Photograph by Ernie Paniccioli

As in all cultures, history serves as a form of empowerment, a reminder of our past to know of our capabilities for a sound and productive future. This song, alone, brings me close to my ancestors, echoing the voice of yesteryear. It is a powerful reminder that we as African Americans have to keep moving. We have to keep working. It tells us that we have to keep our heads to the sky; yet, we must keep our feet firmly planted on the ground.

Every single line of the song is a lesson to be learned. When we were unaware of our thriving civilizations throughout Africa, when we were unaware of Africa's contributions to world history, when we were unaware of ourselves yet able to look forward. It evokes images of the struggle of "the dark past" that takes me back to slavery. I see the pained black faces of a people as they were stolen and rounded up like cattle and transported to Gorée Island, the place of no return. Images when they were thrown into dungeon ships to build the new world of the Americas.

James Weldon Johnson must have been referring to those days of slavery and the atrocious, inhuman conditions like the lynchings, or the displacement of families never to see one another again. He must have been referring to those conditions when he wrote this song in 1900.

As I recite the song today, my mind flashes through our struggles here in America. I see images of four little innocent girls dying from a bomb in a Birmingham, Alabama, church by the hands of ignorant racists. I see my father, Dr. Martin Luther King, Medgar Evers, Nat Turner, Frederick Douglass, Fannie Lou Hamer, Harriet Tubman, Sojourner Truth, and Dr. Betty Shabazz, simply fighting for justice. Further, I see images of too many blacks and too many whites slain victims of bigotry—yet still committed to humanity.

In spite of this nation's flaws regarding race relations, I am still extraordinarily proud of my American heritage. I strive to pay respect and tribute to my ancestors on a daily basis and especially when I hear this song. We have inherited such a powerful tradition in spite of that dark past. Today, we are able to commit ourselves to

*Author Toni Morrison speaking at the launch of the Schomburg Center Capital Campaign, 1987.* Courtesy of Schomburg Center for Research in Black Culture, The New York Public Library

our ancestors and future generations and lift our voice no matter how great the obstacle. We must stay true to ourselves and in doing that stay true to God.

It is a song of faith. It is a song of perseverance. It is a song of triumph!

# GAMILAH-L. SHABAZZ

educator, poet

When asked to contribute to this book, I thought deeply about the song's lyrics. We are living in the new millennium, preparing our youth to understand that the world is truly theirs. With this in mind, I decided to offer a poem that I hope reflects the power and continued strength that we as a people will forever possess, while conquering whatever is placed before us.

*The individual must sort out the distortion of our*
*Racial Consciousness*
*I am blessed, for-I-KNOW*
*I—am the Master—of This*
*Conspiracy Theories*
*Queries of long—ago—*
*Bronzed and booked as fingerprinted*
*Their Spirit's still unsettled—*
*Because—Only—They Know, for the moment . . .*
*MY—BLUEPRINT*
*HUH, —PROOF—OF—IT*
*The SHADOWS That MAKE—Me SEE*
*I will be more than a—*
*Footprint—*
   *In the SAND*
*And those that had had a Hand in the MIX of things*
*Will watch ME——MOVE MOUN-TAINS (YES I CAN, CAN)*
*Wipe the pain away—*

*With—My—Hands*
*Understand dear ANCESTOR,*
*I Can proceed to BE—*
*But if you don't Re-cog-nize*
*And Hand Down*
*THE OTHERS'—LEGACY*
*THEY will have to work on a—Handicap*
*It's OUR WORLD NOW*
*Regroup and send back*
*THEIR MESSAGES*
*Ringing LOUD*
*And in Their Ears . . .*

## MALIK AMJHAAD SHABAZZ

seventh-grade student

This poem is dedicated to those who stood before me: my grand-parents El-Hajj Malik El-Shabazz and Dr. Betty Bahiyah Shabazz; James Weldon Johnson and J. Rosamond Johnson; and the others whose sacrifices made it possible for me to be ready, willing, and able to lift my voice . . .

And for this,
I thank you.

### *Voices and Choices*

*My voice starts as a whisper . . . and then rises with*
*The Others——*
*Rising together So Proud*
*And Strong*
*My ancestors worked for*
*Us now, to have a chance to get where we belong.*
*On our way there*
*We fought and never gave up*

*Enjoying a summer day, 1980s.* Photograph by Ernie Paniccioli

Never ever kneeling down
Or drinking from earth's
Forbidden Cup
We can't stop now
We're almost there
Look up ahead——
    Is that the last Sacred Stair?
As we continue our climb
Don't think I can, but Do
Reaching the top
Is all I feel—I must do.
The Tiger always glares
As I proceed,
But I have a date with Destiny
My ancestors—are Waiting for—ME . . .
I Must make it to the TOP
And sit at the Throne A.K.A. the King's Chair
With the Creator's permission
I will be honored to be there.
We didn't land on Plymouth Rock
Plymouth Rock Landed On You Know Where
Yes, Finally, together We've made it here.
The young ones are still climbing and using their voice to
    get there
And we have to hurry up——
The Beginning—is near
When WE can All come TOGETHER
Like the Lion and the Bear.

*A young boy participates in an NAACP rally against the death penalty, 1990.* Courtesy of the NAACP

# BOBBY SHORT

entertainer

Three or four things in my youth significantly brought together the Negro community in a town where we constituted less than one-tenth the overall population. While Danville, Illinois, could boast of integrated public schools, the local Christian organizations called the YMCA and the YWCA were closed to us. But we had churches, many of them. Churches, it seems, have always been a major force anywhere more than two dozen Negroes are to be found.

Allen Chapel Methodist Episcopal (named for Richard Allen) was located at the north end of town, where a few Negro families had ventured looking for higher ground for themselves and their offspring. Although it was placed at the far end of a street where few Negroes lived, I well recall the weekly trudging back and forth no matter what the weather happened to be. In spite of our minor numbers, Danville also had a chapter of the National Association for the Advancement of Colored People. We took this very seriously, reading *The Crisis* each month and attending meetings whenever possible. The weekly Chicago *Defender* (I was a delivery boy) kept us in touch with the comings and goings of other colored people around the country.

At church, at NAACP meetings, or wherever large numbers of us were assembled at any given time, we all learned to sing the Negro National Anthem, "Lift Every Voice and Sing." The names of the composers, James Weldon Johnson and his brother, J. Rosa-mond Johnson, seemed unreachable and mythlike to me at my tender age, but the upbeat melody and inspiring message of the lyrics came to us all like a delicious balm . . . the kind of balm that singing often produces.

The church's junior choir was masterminded by Miss Cleo Napier, who had enjoyed a career in the entertainment world away from Danville. Miss Napier was more than apt to put snap and bounce into the items she asked her choir to perform. I shall never forget the way she rolled those octaves with her left hand as her group sang out the telling last lines of the anthem, "Facing the rising sun of a new day begun, / Let us march on till victory is won." Not too long ago a major American journalist wrote a provocative piece in which the martial content of some national anthems around the world was pointed out. Much was made of some lines from our own "Star-Spangled Banner," Francis Scott Key's contribution to the nation, in which "the rockets' red glare, the bombs bursting in air" are glorified. But the French took their licks as well. Their beloved but blood-soaked "Marseillaise" winds up with lyrics urging their forces *"Marchons, marchons,"* an order echoed in the Negro National Anthem, in which we are pressed to do likewise. The article brought home the towering fact that "Lift Every Voice and Sing" is a distinctly urgent but basically benign demand for first-class citizenship, and the only anthem of its kind without a call to firearms.

Marching has meant many different things to all of us. We are taught as early as kindergarten to march around the schoolroom; there are parade marches, wedding marches, funeral marches, and so on. The march of the Johnson brothers was its own order. Based militarily solely upon the notion that we are all of us soldiers in the fight for simple equality, it seems less a command than a warm and friendly suggestion that we join hands and move forward together until our goal is ultimately reached, our victory won.

# RODNEY E. SLATER

U.S. secretary of transportation

Working in an Arkansas cotton field as a young boy forty years ago, I was optimistic and full of hope and great expectation. Blame it on youth. I recognize now, however, that the most important things in life were already mine as a God-given birthright—family, commu-

*Camille O. Cosby and Charlayne Hunter-Gault, 1990s.* Photograph by Chris Griffith

nity, and the firm conviction that God created me for his own special purpose. Hope rested on these three pillars, and optimism flowed from their synergy.

Over the years, I have learned that hope is not just for children. It is for all ages. In our small, close-knit community of Marianna, Arkansas, it was as natural to hope and "lift every voice and sing" as it was normal for cotton seeds to sprout or night to follow day. We sang to hope and to remember, to celebrate and to cry, to wish and to offer thanksgiving. We sang when we loved and were loved, and when we felt hurt; we sang of belief and we sang of liberty. We sang "Lift Every Voice and Sing" full-throated, as an anthem, because it celebrates the stony road and the difficult path we have traveled as a people. It is a bittersweet song that echoes with old sorrow, powerful struggle, and the vision of deliverance—the prize that comes from the "steady beat" of sometimes "weary feet" as we move from strength to strength to higher heights.

As the last U.S. transportation secretary of the twentieth century and the first of the twenty-first century, I am struck by how strongly the words of "Lift Every Voice and Sing" evoke transportation as a metaphor for the struggle. Indeed, we call our struggle "the Movement" for good reason. It was on a public transit bus in the year I was born that Rosa Parks was arrested for taking her rightful seat. And it was by leading a bus boycott that the Reverend Martin Luther King, Jr., gave voice to Rosa Parks's cause. We speak of those who fought for open public accommodations as "freedom riders." And we remember as "those who marched" the throngs who came to Washington demanding equal rights as well as those who traversed the Edmund Pettus Bridge and walked from Selma to Montgomery, for the right to vote.

Victory in the new century and the new millennium will be born of our hopes—as we continue to be empowered by the vision and the vigilance expressed by this song, lifting our voices and singing "Till earth and heaven ring / . . . Let our rejoicing rise / High as the listening skies, / . . . Let us march on till victory is won."

*Michael Jordan, 1990s.* Photograph by Ernie Paniccioli

# CHAUNCEY SPENCER

retired business executive

My mother, Anne Spencer, was a poet and educator. Our family home is in Lynchburg, Virginia, where I was born over ninety years ago.

I was fortunate to have known James Weldon Johnson and his wife, Grace. My mother often credited James Weldon Johnson with encouraging her to write and with getting much of her poetry published.

During the 1930s, when Johnson was a professor at Fisk University, he and Mrs. Johnson often spent the night in our home in Lynchburg when they traveled between New York and Nashville, where Fisk University is located. In those days of segregation, there were no hotel accommodations for blacks; therefore, it was a common practice for friends and family to open their homes to weary travelers. Our home was always filled with distinguished guests who stopped for an overnight stay and sometimes even longer: W. E. B. Du Bois, E. Franklin Frazier, Charles Spurgeon Johnson, and Howard Thurman. When our visitors were ready to depart, our family joined them on our front porch, where we held hands and sang "Lift Every Voice and Sing." The song served as a prayer because we knew there was a strong possibility that some catastrophe like death could be waiting down the road for our departing friends as they headed south. "Lift Every Voice and Sing" was the send-off prayer. After we sang the song as loudly as we could lift our voices, our fears were calmed. In those days, no matter what credentials a black man possessed, no matter his station in life, just being black was sufficient to make him a target for lynching.

"Lift Every Voice and Sing" embodies a stirring prayer that my family has long relied on in good and bad times. It is called the Negro National Anthem but it is a song for all peoples who truly seek justice.

# PERCY E. SUTTON

chairman emeritus, Inner City Broadcasting

No prose or poetry could as effectively chronicle the pain and hope in the lives of Africans in America, during the long, long night of slavery and cruelty—and the subsequent years when they were denied justice and equality while suffering subjugation in an apartheid-style system—as do the words of James Weldon Johnson's "Lift Every Voice and Sing."

For one hundred years plus, Africans in America have sung many songs reflecting upon the horrors of slavery, and the American apartheid that followed while expressing hope for "a new day begun."

Unfortunately for us, this "the new day begun" is yet to come.

Even today, there is still evidence that—despite our right to vote, our right to enter eating places and ride public transportation, to enjoy schools and health care and housing—our overall rights to equal treatment, access, and opportunity are too often not enforced without the efforts of the NAACP and likeminded entities.

As I think of this remarkable song, "Lift Every Voice and Sing," which I learned in my childhood in segregated, Jim Crow San Antonio, Texas, I remember how we sang it at home, with my father and mother and brothers and sisters. And we sang it in church, at school, and at virtually every meeting and at every gathering place.

"Lift Every Voice and Sing" was our song of hope for a better future for ourselves, and a strong reminder of our ancestors' long-suffering past. It was the theme song of our lives. We sang it together and we sang it with pride. Indeed, even a handful of undisciplined children, in schoolrooms, often seemed to grasp its sacredness and sang it without blunder.

After I moved to New York as a young military officer, just out of uniform and with high expectations of a different climate of hope and opportunity than had been my experience in Texas, the words of "Lift Every Voice and Sing" took on a more serious and relevant meaning.

*After the parade, 1990s.* Photograph by Chris Griffith

At work, at night, opening the doors of subway trains, or handling mail and baggage as a postal employee, I came to believe that "Lift Every Voice and Sing" was not just about the uplifting of the spirit of a race of people; it was also a clarion call to arms for Americans in general, and African Americans in particular. Its passionate message moved me to become a more aggressive and tireless worker in the battle for justice and equality.

In all of my many years of picket lines, sit-ins, marches, protests, and jailings in the fight for freedom—as a Tuskegee Airman, elected public official, businessman, and lawyer—I have kept with me the clarity of what I believe to have been the purpose of James Weldon Johnson when he wrote: "Thou who hast brought us thus far on the way" and urged us to "march on till victory is won."

I am reminded of friends—the late Malcolm X, Martin Luther King, Jr., and Medgar Evers—and of the many unknown and uncelebrated heroines and heroes of our history, who placed themselves in jeopardy and lost their lives in pursuit of *freedom, justice,* and *equality* for us, and now call out, from the grave: "March on till victory is won."

As this new century begins, all Americans—especially Africans in America—have an obligation to answer the call of "Lift Every Voice" and to "march on till victory is won." The new information society that surrounds us, with its mind-boggling array of wired and wireless communications, high-speed computers, spaceships, laser beams, laser links, microchips, and other devices, requires a skilled and knowledgeable workforce.

We who are able, are commanded to give our all, to move ever forward, to inform, educate, and give access to our brothers and sisters, so that they might also perform, survive, and perhaps even prosper in this new world where information and knowledge are supreme and those without them will fail.

If we do this, we shall not have abandoned the brave and noble legacy we inherited from the heroines and heroes of our past, as we sing, "We have come treading our path through the blood of the slaughtered." And we shall "march on till victory is won."

*Singer Lauryn Hill, 1990s.* Photograph by Ernie Paniccioli

# ELINOR RUTH TATUM

publisher, *The New York Amsterdam News*

I remember, as a little girl, singing the National Anthem and asking myself, "What does it mean to me?" I knew my history and the fact that when independence came, our people were still slaves. Then one day at a dinner in New York City I heard the song "Lift Every Voice and Sing." A light went on in my mind—this song was about me; it was *my* national anthem.

The song tells our history in the manner in which so many of our stories are told. It reaches into the heart and uplifts it. Yet still today there are too few of us who know the true meaning of this song and the need for us to continue our struggle.

As a young woman and journalist living in New York City, I see racism rear its ugly head in many ways: police brutality, inequity in the job market, poor education, inadequate health care, and too many people of color in the prison system. The causes célèbres of the week may come and go, but the struggle remains.

Our fight for freedom and respect did not end in 1863. Our fight did not end in 1964. Our fight did not end with the assassination of Malcolm X in 1965, nor with the assassination of Dr. Martin Luther King, Jr., in 1968. Our fight simply became all the more important, and it continues to be our way of life.

Born in 1971, I did not see the civil rights movement firsthand. I did not walk with Dr. King, as my father did, nor talk with Malcolm X, as my father did, but I have listened to the echo of these conversations. I have listened to some of the greatest thinkers of our time. I have sat at the knee of Dr. John Henrik Clarke, talked to Percy E. Sutton, and supported Charles B. Rangel. I have marched against injustice and spoken out against hate. For as long as I can remember, I have stood up so that all of us can move forward. But at the beginning of this century, I see that our fight against racism and against hate must be put further up on our list of priorities. Our children are not being taught tolerance; hate is

*The Million Man March, October 16, 1995.* Photograph by Chris Griffith

spreading wildly across the Internet. We have to teach our children about our struggle and about our past so that they can make our future brighter.

I know the elders of our community wish the fight were over—and it was supposed to be over, but in actuality every day begins a new struggle. We have come so far. Yet we cannot stop here. There is a light that we must forever reach for. It is time that once again, now and forever, we as a community lift our voices and sing and make it known that we are here, and that we will "march on till victory is won."

## SUSAN TAYLOR

editor in chief, *Essence* magazine

I'd never heard the song in my youth. The anthem wasn't a part of my Caribbean-born parents' experience, nor of mine at the Irish Catholic school and church I attended in Harlem during the 1950s. I never heard "Lift Every Voice and Sing" until the mid-1970s when, as the fashion and beauty editor of *Essence,* I began traveling south to black college campuses to photograph students for the magazine's back-to-school fashion specials. I'll never forget it—seeing scores of beautiful bronze faces lifted toward the sky singing our people's legacy; I felt so deeply the truth and the weight of the words they sang. I remember searching out my own copy of the lyrics, dissecting and digesting them, loving and learning them. Some words from the last stanza have become my mantra, and I often end the speeches I give by asking the audience—regardless of their race or ethnicity—to repeat them after me:

Shadowed beneath Thy hand,
May we forever stand,
True to our God
True to our native land.

"Lift Every Voice and Sing" speaks to the heart of the experience that Diaspora Africans share. Amazingly, James Weldon Johnson was able to write about "the faith that the dark past has taught us" and "the hope that the present has brought us" although odious acts of violence and inhumanity were regularly committed against African Americans in his community. He wrote the anthem in 1900, during the post-Reconstruction Jim Crow era, in Jacksonville, Florida, where black folks had no rights under law that any white person was bound to respect. Johnson's lyrics are a reminder that, even then, the hardest and harshest times were behind our people. Then and now, his words help us put our lives in context and give us the renewed strength of spirit and resolve we need to keep moving forward.

When I sing the words that twenty-nine-year-old James put to his brother Rosamond's music, I remember what we must never forget: that our ancestors were shackled and torn from their motherland, leaving behind all that was familiar and dear to their hearts. That those who paved our way were among the few to survive the trek from the West African hinterland to the coast, the horror of the slave dungeons, the months spent packed in the holds of ships, and the abomination of slavery.

"Lift Every Voice and Sing" is the reminder the world needs that our struggle for civil rights has been a long and painful one—that it didn't begin in the 1950s with sit-ins and demonstrations, with Rosa Parks and Martin Luther King, Jr.; that our battle for black empowerment started long before Malcolm X, Stokely Carmichael, and Angela Davis raised their fists, long before Du Bois, Bethune, and Garvey were even born. Our fight for human rights began centuries ago, with the start of the Atlantic slave trade, when the first Africans decided to rebel because they would rather risk death than be enslaved. "Lift Every Voice and Sing" eloquently and passionately calls us to remember not just our pain, but also the promise that God will never fail us.

The history, the hope, the lessons and faith we must carry with us in order to keep pressing forward—all the things we must

*Jazz musician Wynton Marsalis speaks at an event honoring James Weldon Johnson, New York City, November 19, 1995.*

Courtesy of The James Weldon Johnson Collection, Ollie Jewel Sims Okala, and Sondra Kathryn Wilson

remember—are there, captured in James Weldon Johnson's three pithy verses.

Every time I say the words to our Black National Anthem, I feel renewed and ready again to do battle. Every time I sing those inspiring words, I feel I am rededicating my life to the saneness, wholeness, and forward movement of our people.

## V. MAIA THOMAS

educator and author

As part of the final exam I gave my students, I included a bonus question: Write the first verse of the Negro National Anthem, "Lift Every Voice and Sing." This was an introductory course in African and African American history. We had covered much. But I felt that if my students didn't know this song, if they couldn't feel our struggle, if they didn't understand American racism, then my teaching had been in vain.

I was often troubled, at Afrocentric meetings and conferences, to find that few knew "Lift Every Voice" when asked to sing our anthem. Placed in our chairs were copies of the lyrics, typed and neatly aligned. I could not help but recall that no one passes out the words to "The Star-Spangled Banner." It is taught in the public schools, sung with virtuosity at ball games, patriotic gatherings, and the like. But ours? Who teaches it? Inner-city schools? Black churches? Sororities and fraternities? Our universities? That's why we stand mute or unsure when "Lift Every Voice" is sung. It is not yet ours, because we have failed to embrace it.

So I queried my students, asking if learning the words would infringe on anyone's religious or cultural beliefs. None raised their hands. I left the assignment with them, never discussing it further, but letting them know it would be on the final exam.

Slowly their questions came in: "Professor, which verse did you say we needed to learn?" "Does that include the part that begins 'Sing a song'?" Students began to research the assignment. They

*A parishioner takes a moment to read during church services, 1990s.* Photograph by Chris Griffith

found the anthem on the Internet or in books. They made copies for the class. Some students picked up the sheets with the words to the anthem; others did not.

As promised, I had the question on the test. I watched my students as they took the final exam. Some turned immediately to the bonus question. They wrote the verse feverishly, as though fearing they might forget it. I believed most wanted to answer the question correctly—some, perhaps, for the grade; most because they really felt good knowing it.

"Lift Every Voice," like so much of our history, is unknown to young people. At my church, where we sing the anthem every Sunday, our youth grow up hearing and knowing it. And, I confess, it was here, at this church, that I learned it—at age twenty-five, culturally impoverished despite my academic degrees. Too often, even at my church, we sing "Lift Every Voice" lackadaisically, failing to give it the reverence it deserves. Long-standing church members shake their heads: "If Brother Olawanza were alive, he'd stop the song and make us sing it right!" I never knew our legendary choir director, but somehow I could see him—a giant, little man, vision fading, mind razor sharp—commanding us to sing the anthem until its power and majesty filled our souls.

It warmed my heart to see that most of my students took the question seriously; most tried to write the verse. I was torn: should I mark the answer incorrect if a word or sentence was misplaced? But I didn't. A mere point or two taken off would be enough. Why crush their desire to learn, to know a song that few had taken the time to teach them? I questioned whether I should have made learning "Lift Every Voice" a mandatory part of the exam, not an option. No, I concluded. Let them decide if knowing the anthem was important to them. For only then will they honor it as our song.

It was my goal to teach all our history in one semester—an impossible feat, I soon discovered. By the course's end, I was hoping my students had learned at least one thing they would value throughout their lives. For many, that may have been learning "Lift Every Voice." Now, when they are asked to sing the Negro National Anthem, those young people can pass the neatly typed sheets of paper on to others, perhaps even coach them, teaching the anthem to another generation. They will have the words, even if someone with an ear for music needs to give them the notes. Ask my students to sing "Lift Every Voice," and the majority of them will be able to do so. For that, I am proud; for that, I feel I have been blessed.

## Honor Spingarn Tranum

*artist*

The James Weldon Johnsons were friends of my parents, Amy and Joel Spingarn, for many years. The Johnsons were frequent dinner guests in our home—especially during the summers, because their country house was in Great Barrington, Massachusetts, about thirty miles from our country place in Amenia, New York.

The first time I heard "Lift Every Voice and Sing" was during one of Mr. Johnson's visits to our home in Amenia. Before the Johnsons arrived, Father would sternly remind me and my sister and brothers that we were to remain quiet and listen. "Do not interrupt Mr. Johnson," he insisted. "He is a very knowledgeable man; therefore, listen to him and you will learn." After dinner, Father and Mother usually persuaded Mr. Johnson to read some of his poetry. One Sunday evening, he didn't read but recited the poem "Lift Every Voice and Sing." Being a teenager, I understood the beauty of the poem, but only years later did I realize the full depth of its power.

In early 1933 my father, who was then president of the NAACP, suggested to NAACP executive secretary Walter White and assistant secretary Roy Wilkins that the association should convene a second Amenia conference. (The first one had been held in 1916.) My father's desire was that the conference be held on the grounds of our home, Troutbeck, in Amenia, New York. He wanted to bring together many of the most prominent black leaders of the day, who had differences about the approach to the race problem. Father wanted to have the conference outdoors in the midst of nature, believing that such a setting would have a tempering effect; and that therefore, a degree of unity might be achieved. Tents, tables, sleeping cots, and all things necessary to accommodate our guests for three days were set up on the grounds. At this time I was twenty-three years old. I eagerly looked forward to listening to the speeches, knowing that such notables as Charlie Houston, Roy Wilkins, Ralph Bunche, E. Franklin Frazier, James Weldon Johnson, and W. E. B. Du Bois would be present. This was exciting because I had been too young to attend the first conference but now I was old enough to be involved. During the event I talked to some of the greatest leaders of this century. At the close of the conference we all gathered near a lake to take pictures. Afterwards, we stood holding hands, faced a mountain covered with foliage, and sang "Lift Every Voice and Sing." It was at this time that I was reminded of the evening many years earlier when Mr. Johnson had recited the poem in our home.

Whenever I hear the song today, I often think of something Father said about James Weldon Johnson in 1931: "If a narrow prejudice had not imposed upon him the task of defending a single race, I can imagine him as a shining star among the dim asteroids of the United States Senate."

# WYATT TEE WALKER

minister and civil rights activist

As a lad growing up in the racist environment of southern New Jersey, I might as well have lived in the *real* South. Were the Mason-Dixon line extended east, most of New Jersey where I was reared would have been in the South. The racism I encountered was both overt and subtle. It was overt in that suburban communities such as Oaklyn, six miles across the Delaware River from Philadelphia, posted signs reading "No Colored After Dark." Gloucester, just south of industrial Camden, New Jersey, *did not allow any persons of color to enter the municipality, day or night!* In that social envi-

ronment, I spent the first sixteen years of my life, the tenth child in a preacher's family of eleven.

I was fortunate that my father was a "race man," one who would not allow any white person to diminish his personhood even at the risk of bodily harm. It has always remained significant to me that a large framed photo of Frederick Douglass adorned the wall of our home. The National Association for the Advancement of Colored People has been in my consciousness as long as I can remember. I joined the Youth Council of the NAACP's Camden branch when I was a teenager; hence my early introduction to the musical genius of James Weldon and J. Rosamond Johnson. My entrance into university study came on the wings of "Lift Every Voice and Sing" and I was an active member of the campus chapter of the NAACP at Virginia Union University in Richmond. I can recall participating in a dramatic production with James Edwards, a movie star of the late forties, in a city-wide Richmond benefit. During my college days in Richmond, I walked the city rather than ride on segregated trolley cars. With avid interest I read of Walter White's exploits as the leader of the NAACP in the *Pittsburgh Courier* and other black newspapers. The undergirding dynamic was James Weldon Johnson's hymn, which fired my personal resolve to be a full American citizen. In seminary, I stumbled upon the two volumes of the Johnson brothers' work on Negro spirituals. Those volumes changed my life and ministry. Across the first years of my public and private life James Weldon Johnson became a primary role model though I never met or saw him in life. It was the subliminal influence of "Lift Every Voice and Sing" and the direct influence of Johnson that led me to a career in the study of black sacred music, which culminated in the completion of doctoral study at Rochester Theological Center.

# MAXINE WATERS

## U.S. representative, California

My name is Maxine Waters, but when I sing the Negro National Anthem, I revert to Maxine Carr. Carr is my maiden name. I revert to the little black girl in St. Louis, Missouri, who attended the James Weldon Johnson Elementary School from the fourth to the eighth grade. I feel a special kinship with James Weldon Johnson and the Negro National Anthem. I sang the anthem on days when I trotted to school in the rain and snow without rainwear, boots, or gloves. I sang the Negro National Anthem when I was hungry—I sang the Negro National Anthem when my tooth was hurting because of an exposed cavity—I sang the Negro National Anthem when I did not know there was a future for a little black girl with twelve sisters and brothers. I felt strong when I sang the Negro National Anthem, although I didn't understand the meaning of the words. There was something about those words, and about one of my teachers, Mrs. Stokes, who played the piano as we sang, that just made me feel good.

Each time I rise to sing the Negro National Anthem, I straighten my back, hold my head high, and conjure up my best voice to belt out "Lift every voice and sing / Till earth and heaven ring." The words of the song give me permission to sing loudly and, of course, I sing clearly. I search the room as I sing to see who is singing and who is not. I am a bit contemptuous of the black folks who do not know the words to our own National Anthem, and downright disgusted when it becomes obvious that no one is teaching our young children—they stare at us older folks, who are singing with all our hearts and souls, as if we have lost it! I am also a bit smug about nonblacks who, of course, do not know the words and have that look on their face that says, "Why do all these black folks know this song?" I watch them squirm a bit as they look around and I would like to say to them this is ours, all ours, and it tells the story of how proud we are. We sing of faith and hope. We will not be deterred: "Let us march on till victory is won!"

*A chess player ponders his next move, 1990s.* Photograph by Chris Griffith

I know James Weldon Johnson and his brother wrote this song in 1900 to celebrate the anniversary of Abraham Lincoln's birth, but I feel they wrote it for me, because it expresses my indignation at the perilous journey my people faced on the road to freedom, "Stony the road we trod, / Bitter the chastening rod." It expresses the steadfastness of a people determined to be free no matter the cost. We stayed the course: "Yet with a steady beat, / Have not our weary feet / Come to the place for which our fathers sighed?" Wow! Every word of our precious, beloved Negro National Anthem is so powerful. I love every word of this song—when I sing it, I never fail to get a lump in my throat trying to hold back the tears.

And, finally, the last verse grounds us and teaches us the most important lesson. This verse reminds us not to get too heady and too important, not to forget whence we have come: "Lest our hearts, drunk with the wine of the world, we forget Thee, / Shadowed beneath Thy hand, / May we forever stand, / True to our God / True to our native land." What more does the soul of a black woman need to be renewed? Hope, faith, reflection, courage, steadfastness, godliness, new possibilities—and all derived from our native land, Mother Africa. I do not need any more inspiration than my beloved "Lift Every Voice and Sing." It is the mighty song and the profound description of who we are that guide me in my work, that shape my vision for my people, and that enable me to serve in the Congress of the United States, determined to make this nation and this world what it could be and what it should be. Thank you, James Weldon Johnson.

# JANE WHITE

actress

I'm old now, but whenever I hear "Lift Every Voice and Sing" I'm again filled with my childhood confidence and hope: "Ring with the harmonies of Liberty." I'm eight years old—or ten—or twelve—standing among hundreds of other "colored" people and every one

*Urban cowboy, 1990s.* Photograph by Chris Griffith

of us is perspiring and fanning in an un-air-conditioned auditorium in some Southern city. We're attending an NAACP national conference during a sweltering 1930s summer. My mother, my little brother, and I, all of the people gathered there, are singing at the tops of our voices, garbling some of the words in the middle verses and straining for the high notes, but those words of my "godfather" James Weldon Johnson and his brother's melody tell us that it's eventually going to be a liberated life for us all: "Sing a song full of the hope . . ." And we *believe!*

Perhaps Thurgood Marshall and Charles Houston and other exceptional people are on the dais with the national executive secretary, Walter White. He, my father, will soon report to the conference about battles being fought by the NAACP against brutal lynchings and disenfranchisement and all the other assaults being inflicted upon colored people in this land of freedom. The words he speaks are harsh, but there is flint in my father's eye and in his voice and we know that he and his brave confederates will fight for us until their last breath and that these injustices will not always prevail: "full of the faith that the dark past has taught us." And the music tells us this as it swells and soars and lifts our spirits and makes us feel whole and strong and *together* . . . "till victory is won"!

# LAWRENCE DOUGLAS WILDER

former governor of Virginia

Growing up in America means so many different things to many people. Most Americans have very little appreciation for the effect of growing up in an atmosphere in which race was the most significant part of your everyday life. When, as students in the all-Negro school, we were called upon to stand and sing a song that proclaimed us human and worthy, it was a respite from the toil of self-doubt and legal deprivation. "Lift Every Voice and Sing" was taught and known.

And though there was swelling pride in the airing of the anthem, there was the pathos of reality. For shortly after the last words had wafted through the air, we returned to reality, reminded of what we faced in trying to pursue life, liberty, and happiness. The inspirational words and rhythmic cadence soon subsided. However, for me, there was always the lingering question as to how "hope unborn" could die. I came to know that it's like saying you've got to give chance a chance and that without hope, even as dismal and unrecognizable as it was, all else is lost.

With assaults on the diversity process and the purposeful misconstruing of affirmative action by its critics, we must put the question anew. How do you correct the racial injustices of the past, when privilege and preference were granted to the majority by *legally* confining the minority race to inferior status? We must say to those who object: Call it what you want to, but correct it.

W. E. B. Du Bois predicted that America's problem "is the problem of the color-line." That was said at the start of the twentieth century. Du Bois's prophecy will come into its own in the century we have just entered. We still have those who want full participation in whatever America has to offer. Years of denial, doors slammed in their faces, crosses burned, and violence perpetrated have caused protests and some violent response. When you consider the psychic trauma, little wonder it took so long for the movement against white racism to gather steam and strength. The problem was and is not the rejection of the white majority by minorities, but the rejection of the minority by the white majority.

As we embark on this new millennium, we must not disparage our past but use it for a full appreciation of where we have come from as a people and as a nation. Let us measure the present by the past but project an improvement for the future. We must walk in tandem with those who truly understand that America's destiny is to manage the complex problems of race, free enterprise, and scientific advancements as well as those things that affect us on global levels. To these things, we must commit our fullest resources. We did not do the best that we could have done in the twentieth cen-

*The funeral transport of the casket of Patrick Dorismond amid police-brutality protesters, April 2000.* Photograph by Chris Griffith

tury. If we do not delude ourselves into believing otherwise, then as a nation we can make certain aspects of the dreams and aspirations and the prayers and songs come closer to fulfillment.

## ARMSTRONG WILLIAMS

radio talk-show host, columnist, and political commentator

There are works of art that shed light on an era's particular spirit. For me, one is James Weldon Johnson's "Lift Every Voice and Sing." The song first caught the imagination of African Americans in 1900 as a direct and potent missive to a country where blacks were still regarded largely as cheap labor. Like overlapping church bells, the song evoked the music that poured out of slaves' mouths as they tilled their masters' ruinous landscape. Their words floated upward as their bodies bent beneath sweat and silent tears. One hundred years later, "Lift Every Voice and Sing" endures not only because it evokes the struggle of the African American experience, but also because it speaks to the tortured striving in all of us; it speaks to man's enduring struggle against an often monstrously unjust world.

Three hundred years after these proud Africans were ripped from their culture and deposited in America, their struggle continues. W. E. B. Du Bois said in 1907 that the new century would be the century of race.

*This* century will be a watershed for our country, because it's likely to close with whites in a numerical minority. It's fair to say that the last century has conceived race relations as predominantly between whites and blacks. This century will be far more complex, involving a cluster of different racial and religious groups— Hispanics, Asians, Native Americans, Muslims. And thus finding a harmonious reconciliation between their competing interests will be far more problematic. This will certainly challenge the lofty assertion of Justice Antonin Scalia, in his concurring opinion in *Adarand Construction v. Pena,* that in the United States there's but one race and it is American. The reality is that we have never dealt with a multiplicity of minorities on a national level. At the local level, in places like Los Angeles and Miami, we have witnessed a dress rehearsal, with mixed results; for instance, the predominant use of Spanish in commerce and in culture has awakened latent enmity in whites. And in Los Angeles, competing groups have fought over their share of the quota pie. All these demonstrate that the race issue will be a far more centrifugal force in this century— threatening national unity more than anything has at least since the Civil War.

In this century we must work much harder to develop a fraternal spirit among our population of splintering minorities, if we are to avoid the gruesome and unhappy fate of the Balkans.

Never before have we so urgently needed to imbibe the wisdom of founding father Benjamin Franklin: "We must all hang together, or assuredly we will all hang separately." We will need more politicians of the ilk of Abraham Lincoln and less of the ilk exemplified by extremist factions like the Nation of Islam and the Council of Conservative Citizens.

## Juan Williams

journalist, author, and political commentator

"Lift Every Voice and Sing" is a child's song. It speaks to the child in me. It speaks to my children.

In fact, James Weldon Johnson wrote it for schoolchildren. But even before I knew that it was intended for children, it was obvious to me that the song always reached its highest emotional power in my heart when I heard children sing it. My children began singing it at an all-black elementary school in Washington, D.C. They learned it there as an anthem, sung every morning, a ritual along with the Pledge of Allegiance. The other song they brought home from that school was Bob Marley's liberating "Redemption Song," another paean to the history of the black struggle. But unlike Marley's song, written to be sung by one voice full of haunting loneli-

*Simone plays with her favorite doll, Jennie, May 2000.* Courtesy of the James Weldon Johnson Collection, Sondra Kathryn Wilson

ness and loss, "Lift Every Voice" is a celebration for many voices pulling together, full of evangelical joy, optimism, and faith in America as a land of liberty.

In the high-pitched voices of my children and their classmates, "Lift Every Voice and Sing" was not just a beautiful song but a revelation. It was the children's legacy in song, an inheritance to be passed on to the next generation of African Americans. When I first sang it, as a child, it was a history lesson for me. Here was the story of black people finding themselves in America and making it their home. Here we are, holding our banner high, determinedly marching on, with faith in God, seeking a victory of equality in a land stained by the bitter oppression of legal slavery and segregation.

"Lift Every Voice and Sing" also offers twenty-first-century children of all colors a place in the march of history. The words tell all children how they fit into what Martin Luther King, Jr., called the arc of the struggle for a better world, with a powerful God watching out for them as he did for those who struggled before them.

But as I travel the nation as a writer I notice that the child's experience of the song is the exception, not the rule. Far more commonly, there is an awkward moment when "Lift Every Voice" is sung, especially in front of an adult, interracial audience. Most white Americans do not recognize it as the "Negro Anthem," or even know that there might be such a song. So when some blacks in the audience begin to stand in reverence a question appears on white faces: Is this a black thing—a song of racial separatism and anger?

As a result, when the piano begins that simple, easily recognizable melody and the first few black people stand, soon joined by every other black adult in the room as an expression of solidarity and black consciousness, there is a clear divide. It's not only the whites who sense they are uninitiated in some tradition but also the Hispanics, the Asians, and the Native Americans, as well as the rapidly rising number of recent immigrants. But intuiting that they might be guilty of an unintended slight to those who hold the song close to their hearts, the whites and others begin to pull themselves up one by one.

And once anyone of any race really listens to "Lift Every Voice" and hears the words, with their deep river of faith, their patriotism, and the child's rhymes full of wide-eyed optimism, they never again doubt that there is a powerful emotional need for all to stand and sing out loud.

## SYLVIA WOODS

restaurateur and business executive

Songs like "Swing Low, Sweet Chariot," "Nobody Knows the Trouble I've Seen," "I Come to the Garden Alone," and "Lift Every Voice and Sing" have been spirit lifters and heart warmers in our home for as long as I can remember. I was born in the rural township of Hemingway, South Carolina, where I was raised by my mother, Julia Scott Pressley, and my grandmother, Sylvia Scott. My father died when I was less than two weeks old.

I first remember hearing "Lift Every Voice and Sing" when I was about six, in our family church, Jeremiah Methodist Church, a small white clapboard structure in Hemingway. I noticed the members were singing a bit louder than usual and their voices were filled with a kind of enthusiasm that I didn't understand. Afterward the church was hyped! This song was different because it wasn't our typical church hymn about God and heaven; it was a song about marching on "till victory is won." It was a song about the struggle of our ancestors.

"Lift Every Voice and Sing" was a distinct balm in my childhood, because we were a family of women who lived in perpetual fear for our lives. My maternal grandfather, Robert Scott of Kingstreet, South Carolina, had been lynched in 1906, when my mother was a baby. He had been accused of killing a white grocer. It didn't matter that my grandmother swore on the graves of her ancestors that my grandfather was home the night the grocer was murdered. Their pleading words meant nothing. There was no trial. Grandfather was simply the black man chosen to pay with his life for a crime of which he knew nothing. We always feared that it might happen again.

During the 1930s, as a small child, I would often sit on the floor near the fireplace (where there were invariably a few sweet potatoes roasting in the ashes) and listen to my mother, grandmother, and other female relatives telling stories and singing their "burden-lifting" songs as they quilted. As the women sang the lines "God of our weary years, / God of our silent tears," they would stop quilting. Then in unison, they'd rock their heads back and forth, pat their feet, and clap loudly. Often the women would drop their thimbles and needles and do some shouting across the floor. It seemed as though I heard "a thousand hallelujahs" going up to heaven. These spiritual women would end their ritual by praising God for bringing our family thus far on the way. It was these evenings that eased our fear-filled hearts and minds and wrapped our beings in a soulful balm that I shall not forget as long as I live.

Today, I regularly recall those days in Hemingway, South Carolina, and I am frequently moved to sing those familiar words, "Lift every voice and sing till earth and heaven ring . . ." Then I do a bit of clapping, pat my feet a few times, and rock my head back and forth while praising God Almighty.

## ANDREW YOUNG

former U.S. ambassador to the United Nations

> . . . *Sing*
> *Till earth and heaven ring,*
> *Ring with the harmonies of Liberty.*

No song can compare with this powerful poetic anthem of black America. It is more than a Negro anthem; it is a lyric of freedom with which all humankind can identify.

Freedom's road is indeed stony. There is no freedom without struggle and suffering. Struggles inevitably take you through dark days of doubt and despair, yet perseverance brings us to that Promised Land of our dreams.

Often, almost daily during the 1960s, we mentally rehearsed the words and meanings of our historic struggle. James Weldon Johnson knew well that struggle and entwined its fears and demands with the melodious and certain hope of triumph.

"We Shall Overcome" was always the closing song, expressing the prevailing hope that someday, things would be all right. But "Lift Every Voice and Sing" laid out the road map through tragedy to triumph. For it is the God of our "weary years" and "silent tears" who points the way through the storm, under the rainbow sign. We forget this journey at our peril.

From Montgomery to Memphis, from Atlanta to Africa and into the twenty-first century of promise, we are challenged faithfully to recall this refrain. In church, in the streets, and in the suites, our voices ring with rejoicing.

In the lonely moments of leadership we carry on in the "substance of things hoped for, the evidence of things not seen," refusing to stray from the paths of our historic heroes, knowing that in knowledge and spirit is our true power. We shall overcome, each day.

# POSTSCRIPT

## VERNON E. JORDAN, JR.

*presidential adviser and attorney*

On the wall of my Washington office hangs a photograph of myself with President Bill Clinton. We're standing side by side, singing. Around us are people looking surprised.

That photo is a memento of a very special day. It was taken at a party given by *The Washington Post*'s Katharine Graham at her summer home on Martha's Vineyard in 1993. The guests were various movers and shakers in government and public life, people like Henry Kissinger and Nicholas Katzenbach, among others.

At one point in the evening, the president and I launched into an a cappella duet of the first verse of "Lift Every Voice and Sing." We sang it with feeling, the only way you can sing a song whose poetry is so moving, whose melody is so beautiful, and whose meaning for all black people is so powerful.

Later, the president sent me a copy of that photo and inscribed it: "From the only white man in America who knows all the words." Bill Clinton knew the words because, as a southerner who made racial reconciliation a lifetime goal, they meant much to him. For me, a southerner whose memory bears the marks of the long struggle for equality, that great song also means much.

I first heard it at the Walker Elementary School, where I learned about the song and its authors. Every year, my parents would take me to the Atlanta NAACP's Emancipation Day program, where the song was sung and where I was enraptured by it.

By the seventh grade, I had memorized it. I played it as a member of my high school band. I have quoted it often in my public speeches. I have used its third verse as a prayer, which it is. I have referred to it as a song that embodies the dreams and aspirations of black Americans. Since it was written a century ago it has given us hope and faith; it has embodied our love of our country, our faith in our God, and our pride in our past.

That's why I always get a thrill from hearing it and a charge from singing it. It is part of me now. I am imprinted with its melody, which touches the heart, and its poetry, which touches the soul and the mind.

# AFTERWORD

## KWEISI MFUME

### president and CEO, NAACP

James Weldon Johnson's "Lift Every Voice and Sing" has become the eminently celebrated anthem for African Americans as we continue to journey through the labyrinth of sociopolitical and economic challenges. The incessant reminder of life's exclusions and judgments of our people makes the glory and affection of this special song that much more significant to our heritage. As we begin to adjust ourselves to the new racial challenges of this century, we pledge to masterfully circumvent our foes and regain our rightful place in this nation. It is our anthem, our signature expression of freedom, which drives us with uninterrupted pride to reach our goals.

Thus we must become, among other things, economically empowered. It is no secret that the greatest impediment to economic development in communities of color is a lack of access to capital and credit. The racial considerations we faced forty years ago are now clouded with class considerations. Despite the changes in this country, it is undeniable that too many people still live in poverty, and that the prosperity enjoyed by many in this nation is hardship for many others. People of color across this nation who are part of the working poor continue to fall further behind.

We must remind ourselves and the larger American public of our power within this nation. Boycotts and demonstrations have been extraordinarily effective in the past, and are equally important today. These examples of coordinated action still resonate, because in a capitalistic society, profit and loss are what matter most, and because right-minded people continue to be moved by meaningful protests against the wrongheaded evils of bigotry and intolerance. We must rise to every occasion, wielding the considerable power that we possess, and we must do so without apology.

Demographers suggest that by the year 2040, there will not be any majority group in this nation. This fact clearly illustrates that even if some Americans do not embrace change, they will be overtaken by it. We are a nation blessed—after a tumultuous history— to have within our midst different groups of people whose collective and individual diversity add to the American experience and to our ability to effect real change.

We must force our government to enforce the law. In an era prolific with judicial reinterpretation of laws dealing with civil rights and affirmative action, we must stand fast as citizens and voters to halt any "redefinition" of basic statutes. Such statutes have helped to guarantee what measure of equality we have achieved over the years. We must call extensive attention to the dire need for full voter empowerment—proportionate voter participation, appropriate political education, and thorough voter turnout—within communities of color. One of the most crucial actions we can take is to organize our collective strength into an effective electoral force to put extra pressure on the decision makers in an effort to address a broad range of concerns. In order to live in an America that is truly a nation for, by, and of the people, we must become active and responsible members of the political process who vote, lobby, and campaign to ensure that rights are protected.

We have to find new ways to do more and to be more to our young people. They are not Generation "X," signifying the unknown; they are ours—all of them. As such, they are also our responsibility. Many of the young men and women among us rightfully feel that they have the capacity to shape their futures. They must never be made to feel that they are powerless to effect meaningful change in their lives or in their society. For those of us who have fewer days to live than the number of days we have already lived, our young people are the renewal of life and the embodiment of our struggle. Ignorance remains the enemy of self-reliance. We must therefore empower our young people with both education and values, as they are the ones who will ultimately empower us.

We must renew our emphasis on the things that work: fighting for our dignity; defining ourselves; rebuilding our communities; and taking personal ownership of our lives, our values, and our families. We must ultimately find a way to rise beyond ourselves, beyond our conditions, and find the courage to make the painful sacrifices so desperately needed. Such selflessness will not only nourish our human spirit, but also will elevate our communities and empower our nation. Let us therefore commit ourselves from this day forward to vote in greater numbers, speak in louder voices, write with sharper pens, and act with firmer convictions.

*Facing the rising sun of our new day begun,*
*Let us march on till victory is won.*

# James Weldon Johnson: A Chronology

1871    Born June 17 to James and Helen Louise Dillet Johnson in Jacksonville, Florida.

1884    Makes trip to New York City.

1886    Meets Frederick Douglass in Jacksonville.

1887    Graduates from Stanton School in Jacksonville. Enters Atlanta University Preparatory Division.

1890    Graduates from Atlanta University Preparatory Division. Enters Atlanta University's freshman class.

1891    Teaches school in Henry County, Georgia, during the summer following his freshman year.

1892    Wins Atlanta University Oratory Prize for "The Best Methods of Removing the Disabilities of Caste from the Negro."

1893    Meets Paul Laurence Dunbar at the Chicago World's Fair.

1894    Receives B.A. degree with honors from Atlanta University. Delivers valedictory speech, "The Destiny of the Human Race." Tours New England with the Atlanta University Quartet for three months. Is appointed principal of Stanton School in Jacksonville, Florida, the largest African American public school in the state.

1895    Founds the *Daily American,* an afternoon daily serving Jacksonville's black population.

1896    Expands Stanton School to high school status, making it the first public high school for blacks in the state of Florida.

1898    Becomes the first African American to be admitted to the Florida bar.

1900    Writes the lyrics to "Lift Every Voice and Sing" with music by his brother, J. Rosamond Johnson. Meets his future wife, Grace Nail, in New York.

1901    Elected president of the Florida State Teachers Association. Nearly lynched in a Jacksonville park. This near lynching made him realize that he could not advance in the South.

1902    Resigns as principal of Stanton School. Moves to New York to form musical trio—Cole and the Johnson Brothers. As part of this trio he writes over 200 popular songs, many of which are used in Broadway productions.

1903    Attends graduate school at Columbia University, where he studies with Brander Matthews, professor of dramatic literature.

1904    Writes two songs for Theodore Roosevelt's presidential campaign. Becomes a member of the National Business League, an organization founded by Booker T. Washington. Receives honorary degree from Atlanta University. During this time he meets W. E. B. Du Bois, then a professor at Atlanta University.

1905    Cole and the Johnson Brothers go on European tour. Becomes president of Colored Republican Club in New York City.

1906    Accepts membership in the American Society of International Law. Is appointed U.S. consul to Venezuela by President Theodore Roosevelt.

1909    Is promoted to U.S. consul to Corinto, Nicaragua.

1910    Marries Grace Elizabeth Nail, daughter of well-known Harlem businessman John Bennett Nail, on February 3, in New York City.

1912    Publishes anonymously *The Autobiography of an Ex-Colored Man*, probably the earliest first-person fictional narrative by an African American.

1913    Resigns from the consular service on account of race prejudice and party politics.

1914    Accepts position as contributing editor to the *New York Age*. Becomes a founding member of the American Society of Composers, Authors and Publishers (ASCAP). Joins Sigma Pi Phi fraternity and Phi Beta Sigma fraternity.

1915    Becomes member of the NAACP. Puts into English the libretto of *Goyescas,* the Spanish grand opera, which is produced at the Metropolitan Opera House.

1916    Attends the NAACP conference in Amenia, New York, at the estate of J. E. Spingarn. Delivers speech, "A Working Programme for the

Future." Joins the staff of the NAACP in the position of field secretary.

1917    Publishes volume *Fifty Years and Other Poems*. Publishes poem "Saint Peter Relates an Incident of the Resurrection Day." With W. E. B. Du Bois, leads over 12,000 marchers down New York's Fifth Avenue to protest lynchings and riots. Becomes acting secretary of the NAACP. Supports U.S. entry into World War I and fights against the atrocities perpetrated against black soldiers. Meets Walter White in Atlanta and persuades him to join the staff of the NAACP. Attends conference of the Intercollegiate Socialist Society in Bellport, New York; gives talk on the contribution of the Negro to American culture. With W. E. B. Du Bois, becomes charter member of the Civic Club, a liberal club that grew to be a strong influence in the life of black New Yorkers.

1918    Is responsible for an unprecedented increase in NAACP membership in one year, particularly in the South, making the NAACP a national power.

1919    Participates in converting the National Civil Liberties Bureau into a permanent organization, the American Civil Liberties Union.

1920    NAACP board of directors names him secretary (chief executive officer), making him the first African American to serve in that position. Publishes "Self-Determining Haiti," which draws on his earlier investigation of the American occupation there.

1922    Publishes *The Book of American Negro Poetry*.

1924    Assists several writers of the Harlem Renaissance.

1925    Receives the NAACP's Spingarn Medal. Coauthors, with J. Rosamond Johnson, *The Book of American Negro Spirituals*.

1926    Coauthors, with J. Rosamond Johnson, *The Second Book of American Negro Spirituals*. Purchases an old farm in the Massachusetts Berkshires and builds a summer cottage called Five Acres.

1927    During the height of the Harlem Renaissance, *The Autobiography of an Ex-Coloured Man* is reprinted. (The spelling "coloured" was used to enhance British sales.) *God's Trombones* is published.

1928    Receives Harmon Award for *God's Trombones*. Receives D. Litt. from Howard University and Talladega College.

1929    Takes a leave of absence from the NAACP. Attends the Third Japanese Biennial Conference on Pacific Relations. Receives Julius Rosenwald Fellowship to write *Black Manhattan.*

1930    *Black Manhattan,* the story of African Americans in New York from the seventeenth century to the 1920s, is published.

1931    Publishes the revised and enlarged edition of *The Book of American Negro Poetry.* NAACP honors him by hosting a testimonial dinner in New York City attended by over 300 guests. Is appointed vice president and board member of the NAACP. Accepts Fisk University appointment as the Adam K. Spence Professor of Creative Literature.

1933    Publishes autobiography, *Along This Way.* Attends the second NAACP Amenia Conference.

1934    Is appointed visiting professor, fall semester, at New York University, becoming the first African American to hold such a position at the institution. Receives the Du Bois Prize for *Black Manhattan* as the best book of prose written by an African American during a three-year period. Publishes *Negro Americans, What Now?*

1935    Publishes *Saint Peter Relates an Incident: Selected Poems.*

1938    Dies June 26 as a result of an automobile accident in Wiscassett, Maine, nine days after his sixty-seventh birthday. Funeral held at the Salem Methodist Church in Harlem on Thursday, June 30. Is cremated.

*Mrs. James Weldon Johnson (Grace Nail Johnson) died on November 1, 1976. Grace and James Weldon Johnson were interred together by Ollie Jewel Sims Okala on November 19, 1976, in the Nail family plot in Green-Wood Cemetery, Brooklyn, New York.*

# J. ROSAMOND JOHNSON:
## A CHRONOLOGY

1873  Born August 4 to James and Helen Louise Dillet Johnson in Jacksonville, Florida.

1890  Enters the New England Conservatory in Boston, Massachusetts.

1896  Returns to Jacksonville. Becomes choirmaster and organist for Bethany Baptist Church.

1897  Makes acting debut in John Isham's *In Oriental America,* the first African American show to appear on Broadway.

1899  Spends summer in New York and meets important figures in the music business such as Isadore Witnaek, Harry B. Smith, and Reginald de Koven.

1900  Writes the music to "Lift Every Voice and Sing." Establishes partnership with vaudevillian Robert "Bob" Cole. The duo becomes known as Cole and Johnson.

1902  James Weldon Johnson joins Cole and Johnson; the group is now called Cole and the Johnson Brothers.

1905  Cole and the Johnson Brothers go on European tour.

1912  Becomes director of Oscar Hammerstein's Grand Opera House in London.

1913  Marries Nora Ethel Floyd of Jacksonville, Florida, on July 13 in London.

1914  Daughter Mildred Louise is born on May 25.

1916  Founds the New York Music School Settlement for Colored People in Harlem.

1917  Receives honorary master's degree from Atlanta University.

1925  Writes the musical arrangements for *The Book of American Negro Spirituals.*

1926  Writes the musical arrangements for *The Second Book of American Negro Spirituals.*

1931	Contracts with the Handy Brothers Music Company, Inc., to publish a collection of spirituals.

1935	Plays leading roles in the original cast of *Porgy and Bess.*

1937	Writes the musical arrangements for the book *Rolling Along.*

1954	Dies November 11, at home in New York City. Is buried in Mount Hope Cemetery, Hartsdale, New York.

# BIBLIOGRAPHY

## Works by James Weldon Johnson

*Along This Way: The Autobiography of James Weldon Johnson.* New York: Viking Press, 1933. Reprinted with an introduction by Sondra Kathryn Wilson, New York: Da Capo Press, 2000.

*The Autobiography of an Ex-Colored Man.* Boston: Sherman, French & Co., 1912. Reprinted, New York: Penguin Classics, 1990. Reprinted with an introduction by Henry Louis Gates, Jr., New York: Alfred A. Knopf, 1990.

*Black Manhattan.* New York: Alfred A. Knopf, 1930. Reprinted with an introduction by Sondra Kathryn Wilson, New York: Da Capo Press, 1991.

*Fifty Years and Other Poems.* Boston: Cornhill Publishers, 1917.

*God's Trombones: Seven Negro Sermons in Verse.* New York: Viking Press, 1927. Reprinted, New York: Penguin Classics, 1990. Produced on audio by Sondra Kathryn Wilson for Penguin-Highbridge, 1993.

*Negro Americans, What Now?* New York: Viking Press, 1934.

*Saint Peter Relates an Incident: Selected Poems* (also titled *Lift Every Voice and Sing*). New York: Viking Press, 1935. Reprinted with a preface by Sondra Kathryn Wilson, New York: Penguin Putnam, 2000.

*The Book of American Negro Poetry,* edited by James Weldon Johnson. New York: Harcourt Brace and World, 1922. Reprinted, New York: Harcourt Brace Jovanovich, 1969.

## Works by James Weldon Johnson and J. Rosamond Johnson

*The Book of American Negro Spirituals,* edited by James Weldon Johnson and J. Rosamond Johnson. New York: Viking Press, 1925. Reprinted, New York: Da Capo Press, 1989.

*The Second Book of American Negro Spirituals,* edited by James Weldon Johnson and J. Rosamond Johnson. New York: Viking Press, 1926. Reprinted, New York: Da Capo Press, 1989.

## Secondary Sources

Adelman, Lynn. "A Study of James Weldon Johnson." *Journal of Negro History* 52 (April 1967): 128–45.

Akar, John J. "An African View of Black Studies with International Dimensions." *CLA Journal* 14 (1970): 7–18.

Aptheker, Herbert. "Du Bois on James Weldon Johnson." *Journal of Negro History* 52 (1967): 224–27.

Bacote, Clarence A. "James Weldon Johnson and Atlanta University." *Phylon* 32 (winter 1971): 333–43.

Baker, Houston. "A Forgotten Prototype: *The Autobiography of an Ex-Colored Man* and *Invisible Man.*" In *Singers of Daybreak,* edited by Houston Baker. Washington, D.C.: Howard University Press, 1974.

Barksdale, Howard Reed. "James Weldon Johnson as a Man of Letters." Master's thesis, Fisk University, 1936.

Bone, Robert. *The Negro Novel in America.* New Haven: Yale University Press, 1965.

Bontemps, Arna, editor. *The Harlem Renaissance Remembered.* New York: Dodd Meade, 1972.

Braithwaite, William Stanley. "A Review of the Autobiography of James Weldon Johnson." *Opportunity* 11 (1933): 376–78.

Bronz, Stephen H. *Roots of Negro Racial Consciousness, the 1920's: Three Harlem Renaissance Authors.* New York: Libra Publishers, 1964.

Canady, Nicholas. "*The Autobiography of an Ex-Colored Man* and the Traditions of Black Biography." *Obsidian* 6 (spring–summer 1980): 76–80.

Carroll, Richard A. "Black Racial Spirit: An Analysis of James Weldon Johnson's Critical Perspective." *Phylon* 32 (winter 1971): 344–64.

Clark, Peter W. "A Study of the Poetry of James Weldon Johnson." Master's thesis, Xavier University, 1942.

Collier, Eugenia. "The Endless Journey of an Ex-Colored Man." *Phylon* 32 (winter 1971): 365–73.

———. "James Weldon Johnson: Mirror of Change." *Phylon* 21 (fourth quarter, 1960): 351–59.

Copans, Sim J. "James Weldon Johnson et le patrimonie culturel des noirs africains." *Cahier de la compagnie Madeleine Renaud–Jean Louis Barrault* 61 (1967): 422–48.

Davis, Arthur P. *From the Dark Tower: Afro-American Writers 1900 to 1960.* Washington, D.C.: Howard University Press, 1974.

Fleming, Robert E. "Contemporary Themes in Johnson's *Autobiography of an Ex-Colored Man.*" *Negro American Literature Forum* 4 (winter 1970): 120–124, 141.

———. "Irony as a Key to Johnson's *The Autobiography of an Ex-Colored Man.*" *American Literature* 43 (March 1971): 83–86.

Gates, Henry Louis, Jr. *Thirteen Ways of Looking at a Black Man.* New York: Vintage Books, 1998.

———and Nellie Y. McKay, et al., editors. *The Norton Anthology of African American Literature.* New York: W. W. Norton, 1997.

Huggins, Nathan Irvin. *Harlem Renaissance.* New York: Oxford University Press, 1971.

Jackson, Miles, Jr. "James Weldon Johnson." *Black World* 19 (June 1970): 32–34.

———. "Literary History: Documentary Sidelights, James Weldon Johnson and Claude McKay." *Negro Digest* 17 (June 1968): 25–29.

Kostelanetz, Richard. "The Politics of Passing: The Fiction of James Weldon Johnson." *Negro American Literature Forum* 3 (March 1969): 22–24, 29.

Levy, Eugene. *James Weldon Johnson: Black Leader, Black Voice.* Chicago: University of Chicago Press, 1973.

———. "James Weldon Johnson." In *Black Leaders of the Twentieth Century,* edited by John Hope Franklin and August Meier. Chicago: University of Chicago Press, 1980.

Lewis, David Levering. *When Harlem Was in Vogue.* New York: Oxford University Press, 1989.

———, editor. *The Portable Harlem Renaissance Reader.* New York: Viking Penguin, 1994.

Logan, Rayford W., and Michael R. Winston, editors. *Dictionary of Negro Biography.* New York: W. W. Norton, 1981, 353–57.

Long, Richard A. "A Weapon of My Song: The Poetry of James Weldon Johnson." *Phylon* 32 (winter 1971): 374–82.

Mason, Julian. "James Weldon Johnson." In *Fifty Southern Writers After 1900,* Joseph M. Flora and Robert Bian, editors, 280–89. New York: Greenwood Press, 1987.

Miller, Ruth, and Peter J. Katopes. "The Harlem Renaissance: Arna Bontemps, Countee Cullen, James Weldon Johnson, Claude McKay, and Jean Toomer." In *Black American Writers: Bibliographical Essays.* Vol. 1: *The Beginnings Through the Harlem Renaissance and Langston Hughes,* Thomas Inge, et al., editors, 161–206. New York: St. Martin's Press, 1978.

Millican, Arthenia Bates. "James Weldon Johnson: In Quest of an Afrocentric Tradition for Black American Literature." Ph.D. diss., Louisiana State University, 1972.

O'Sullivan, Maurice J. "Of Souls and Pottage: James Weldon Johnson's *The Autobiography of an Ex-Colored Man*." *CLA Journal* 23 (September 1979): 60–70.

Ovington, Mary White. *The Walls Came Tumbling Down: The Autobiography of Mary White Ovington, a Founder of the N.A.A.C.P.* New York: Schocken Books, 1947.

Price, Kenneth M., and Lawrence J. Oliver, editors. *Critical Essays on James Weldon Johnson.* New York: G. K. Hall, 1997.

Redding, J. Saunders. *To Make a Poet Black.* Chapel Hill: University of North Carolina Press, 1939. Reprinted, College Park, Md.: McGrath Publishing Co., 1968.

Rosenblatt, Roger. *"The Autobiography of an Ex-Colored Man,"* in *Black Fiction.* Cambridge, Mass.: Harvard University Press, 1974.

Sanquist, Eric J. *The Hammers of Creation: Folk Culture in Modern African-American Fiction.* Mercer University, 1993.

Skerrett, Joseph T., Jr. "Irony and Symbolic Action in James Weldon Johnson's *The Autobiography of an Ex-Colored Man*." *American Quarterly* 32 (winter 1980): 540–48.

Starke, Catherine Juanita. *Black Portraiture in American Fiction: Stock Characters, Archetypes, and Individuals.* New York: Basic Books, 1971.

Whitlow, Roger. *Black American Literature: A Critical History.* Chicago: Nelson-Hall, 1973.

Wilson, Sondra Kathryn, with Warren Marr. *Paying for Freedom: The Story of the N.A.A.C.P. Life Membership Program.* New York: NAACP Press, 1988.

Wilson, Sondra Kathryn. "James Weldon Johnson." *The Crisis,* January 1989: 48–51, 117, 118.

———, guest editor. "Collected Writings of James Weldon Johnson." *Langston Hughes Review* 7 (spring/fall 1989).

———, editor. *The Selected Writings of James Weldon Johnson,* Vols. 1 and 2. New York: Oxford University Press, 1995.

———, editor. *The* Crisis *Reader: Stories, Poems, and Essays from the NAACP's* Crisis *Magazine.* New York: Modern Library, 1999.

———, editor. *In Search of Democracy: The NAACP Writings of James Weldon Johnson, Walter White, and Roy Wilkins (1920–1977).* New York: Oxford University Press, 1999.

———, editor. *The Collected Poetry of James Weldon Johnson.* New York: Penguin Putnam, 2000.

Wohlforth, Robert. "Dark Leader: James Weldon Johnson." *The New Yorker,* September 30, 1933, 20–24.

Young, James O. *Black Writers of the Thirties.* Baton Rouge: Louisiana State University Press, 1973.

## Collections

The James Weldon Johnson Papers in the James Weldon Johnson Memorial Collection of Negro Arts and Letters, Beinecke Library, Yale University, New Haven, Connecticut.

The James Weldon Johnson Papers in African American Collections, Woodruff Library, Emory University, Atlanta, Georgia.

ABOUT THE TYPE

This book was set in Fairfield, the first typeface from the hand of the distinguished American artist and engraver Rudolph Ruzicka (1883–1978). In its structure Fairfield displays the sober and sane qualities of the master craftsman whose talent has long been dedicated to clarity. It is this trait that accounts for the trim grace and vigor, the spirited design and sensitive balance, of this original typeface.